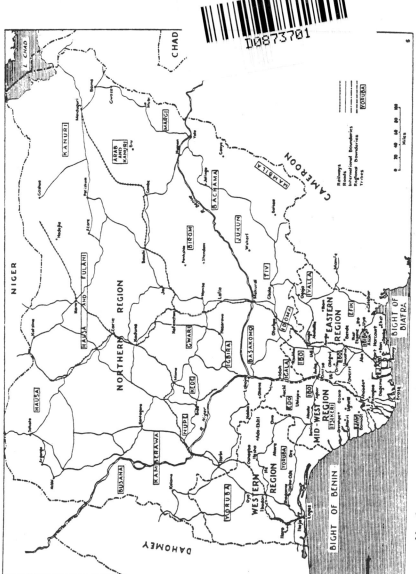

Map 2-1 • Nigeria, January 1966 (from John de St. Jorre, *The Nigerian Civil War*, front endpaper.)

A Song of Africa

by

Ronald B. Wheatley

Cover Design by Elizabeth Herron Wheatley

ISBN: 1-4635-1179-5
ISBN-13: 9781463511791

For Ethel

"If I know a song of Africa, - I thought – of the Giraffe, and the African new moon lying on her back, of the poughs in the fields, and the sweaty faces of the coffee pickers, does Africa know a song of me? Would the air over the plain quiver with a colour that I had on, or the children invent a new game in which my name was, or the full moon cast a shadow over the gravel of the drive that was like me, or would the eagles of Ngong look out for me?"

Isak Dinncson

"Out of Africa"

PROLOGUE

Before there was a military government in Nigeria, before there was a Federal Republic of Nigeria, before there was a Conference of Berlin, before there was a jihad, before there was the first European explorer or missionary, there were the Sudan, the peoples, and the great Niger River. With its mouth, a massive network of capillaries feeding the seemingly limitless mangrove from the Bight of Benin on the west to the Bight of Biafra on the east, the river has flowed for centuries.

To a large extent the natural boundaries established by the course of the river dictated not only the habitat of the ethnic groups or tribes of the land contiguous to it, the Hausa-Fulanis of the north, the Yorubas of the West and the Ibos of the East, but their social, economic, cultural, and religious practices, as well as their relationship with their neighbors in other parts of the land. Within these natural divisions the indigenous peoples' societies developed, generally, in an insular, segmented fashion that focused first on the most narrow segments of the society, the family and the extended family, clan and tribe, but not generally beyond.

At the beginning of the nineteenth century the Hausa-Fulanis States of the North were controlled by pagan rulers. The minority of devout Moslems in the North suffered under this leadership which they considered both politically oppressive and morally decadent.

It was at this time that an itinerate devout Islamic scholar, Uthman dan Fodio, through his proselytizing, began to unify the suffering minority of the followers of Islam. As the movement grew, it soon became apparent that the spread of the faith was considered by the pagan oppressors as a threat to their way of life, a threat which would be put down by force. Seeing no other alternative to achievement of the goals of preserving the religious conversions which he had accomplished and the further growth of Islam in the area, Uthman declared himself the Amin al-Muminin, the Commander of the Faithful, and proclaimed a jihad, a holy war, against non-believers. Through the popularity of the cause, the charisma of the man, and the religious zeal of the time, the jihad spread the "new" religion throughout Northern Sudan, uniting the Hausa States in a secular and religious structure which through sheer numbers would eventually be the dominant political force in the then inchoate nation.

Yet, whereas Ilsam was successful in uniting the Hausa States in the north, this was not the case in the West where the Yorubas predominated, nor in the East which was the home of the Ibo nation. In fact, in the West quite the contrary happened, for although the Jihad had penetrated the area and an Islamic presence became firmly established there, it did not lead to the kind of unification of the peoples that occurred in the North. The presence of the ancient Oyo Empire of the Yorubas helped to halt the spread of Islam in the West. Yet the Jihad did lead eventually to the collapse of the Oyo

Empire, which in turn led to a series of civil wars among the Yorubas during the last half of the nineteenth century, ending finally in the Yoruba states entering into peace treaties under British protection.

The Ibos were even less affected by the Jihad because the rain forests of the East were a natural barrier to Uthman's cavalry. Although the Ibo nation was a segmented society comprised of numerous clans, the Ibo people were more successful in avoiding civil strife by resorting to an Oracle system to settle disputes. Once under British influence the Ibo clan system was quite adaptable to amalgamation into Nigeria. They were influenced by the Christian missionaries that had penetrated the coast and they quickly adapted their cooperative clan system to western modern ways. The western missionaries, particularly the Roman Catholic missionaries, understood the cooperative spirit of this movement, and they were quick to take advantage of it. A symbiotic relationship was established and by late nineteenth century the Ibos were emerging in the new Nigerian political life in a way that was unparalleled by other tribes in the country.

As it did with its other colonial possessions, the British used the system of Indirect Rule in Nigeria. Nigeria, with its three major regions each dominated by a different ethnic group, was particularly amenable to such colonial rule. The British capitalized on this diversity and by playing on rival factions were able to perpetuate their own dominance in the colony.

In 1900, the British Government took control over the Coast Protectorate, which resulted in the birth of Nigeria. Between 1912 and 1919, the northern and southern regions of the country were united by the British, and in 1914, the Protectorate of Nigeria was officially recognized. In 1960, the country became independent.

But what the river in its centuries-long march to the sea had accomplished, in dividing the three great peoples and the countless minority tribes, could not be undone by Jihads or by drawing some lines on a map of Africa at the Berlin Conference, in 1895, when the European countries were scrambling for the riches of these African nations and calling them countries, and claiming them for themselves, or even by a colonial presence.

As a result, when the country approached independence in the heady days when the "winds of change" were sweeping the continent, there was no course of national unity rising above narrower tribal loyalties, there was only the course set by the great river.

AUTHOR'S NOTE

On January 15, 1966, in the cool, early morning blackness of Kaduna, the desert capitol of Northern Nigeria,
a small cadre of young Federal Nigerian Army officers
scaled the low wall surrounding Nassarawa Lodge, the
palace of Sir Abmadu Bello, the Sardauna of Sokoto and
Premier of the Northern Region. The raid, like the others
which Major Chukwuma Nzeogwu had led the past
few nights, was believed by his troops to be a train-
ing maneuver. Major Nzeogwu was a Sandhurst educated
Ibo and brilliant instructor from the Nigerian Defense
Academy. The major had waited until the last moment
to inform his compatriots of his true intention that this
indeed would be no drill. He revealed the plan knowing
that, in doing so, he risked everything. He had no gun,
though the others carried automatics. Had they wished
they could have cut him down as a traitor, but they did
not. In the dark silence they set up the antitank gun
which they had checked out from the armory, and aimed
it at pointblank range at the palace. The black velvet
stillness of the pre-dawn hours was suddenly shattered
as they began blasting away at the palace. It only took
a few rounds to blow away most of the roof of the building. Then the Major rushed the front doors of the lodge,
he had to use a hand grenade to blast them open, and

he was himself seriously wounded by its shrapnel. His troops stormed the palace and immediately undertook a room-to-room search, finally finding the Sardauna hiding with the women of his harem. As the soldiers dragged him across the room in his pajamas, some of the women tried to protect the great man. Furious, the soldiers slammed the Sardauna against the wall and shot him dead. By that act they assassinated the most powerful man in Nigeria, the most populous country in Africa, and set into place a chain of events which would lead to civil war in the country, and to what many would come to believe to be the attempted genocide of the Ibo people.

As Premier of the North, Ahmadu Bello was both a secular and religious leader, but he was more. He was the symbol of the Hausa-Fulani political domination of Nigeria. Just as important was the fact that Major Nzeogwu happened to be an Ibo. His assassination was the match to the dry kindling of tribal hatred between the less progressive, almost feudal Hausa-Fulanis of the North who by sheer numbers dominated the politics of the entire country and the dynamic and modernized Ibos of the Eastern part of the country.

Strategically, throughout the country, other dissident Federal troops were assassinating other Northern military and political officers, including: the Prime Minister and statesman, Alhadji Sir Abubakar Tafawa Balewa, the Consummate Election Rigger, Samual Akintola, the Premier of the Mid-Western Region, and the corrupt Minister of Finance. The President of Nigeria, Dr. Nnamdi Azikwe, was by most accounts spared only because he happened to be out of the country at the time of the assassinations which ended the most ambitious experiment to date in the operation of a parliamentary democratic government in Africa based on the Western system. The deaths of Balewa and Bello, particularly, ended an era in Africa which may become more sweeping in its aftermath than the end of the era of colonization.

In the ecstatically cataclysmic days immediately following the coup, Major General Aguiyi-Ironsi, an Ibo and then Chief of Staff of the Federal Nigerian Army, swore his allegiance to the Federal Government, and was appointed leader of the newly established military government. One of the most urgent initial acts of the new military government, was the appointing of military governors for the now four regions of the country, which were then changed to provinces, North, East, Midwest, and West. Two such appointments, later to have a major impact on the country, were those of the governor of the Eastern region, an Ibo and Christian, Lt. Col. Chukwuemeku Odumegwu Ojuwku, and Lt. Col. Yakabu Gowon, a Christian, from the small Argas tribe located on the Jos Plateau, who was made the army chief of staff.

Six months later, General Ironsi was dead, assassinated July 29, 1966, by those opposed to his policy of establishing a unitary state. The majority of the Northerner Hausa-Fulani Moslems were afraid of being ruled by the Southern and Christian Ibos. Yakabu Gowon emerged as the country's new military leader.

On "Black Thursday," Nigeria, September 29, 1966, thousands of Ibo middle class shopkeepers and civil servants who were working in the North were slaughtered in Northern inspired, anti-Ibo riots. According to some reports, as many as 50,000 Ibos died in the pogrom, and a mass exodus of Ibos from that area began. Those who survived, and those who made it back to their homeland in the Eastern Region, recounted traumatic tales of the horror.

On May 27, 1967 the new leader of Nigeria, in an attempt to splinter the existing regional, ethnic and religious power blocs, further divided the four provinces of the country into twelve states.

The seeds of national disintegration had been planted many years before, but these two coups hastened the event. On May 30, 1967, less than a year after the second coup, the then self-proclaimed General Ojukwu, seeing no hope of reconciliation, declared secession of the Eastern Region and the establishment of the "Republic of Biafra." The Federal Government denounced the act of secession as rebellion and sent troops to attack Biafra. By early July, the country was plunged into a bloody civil war which was to last two and a half years causing onlookers to believe its ultimate objective was becoming the genocide of the Ibo people.

Perhaps the most crucial battle of the war was launched on August 9, 1967, just a few months following Ojukwu's declaration of independence, when Biafran troops launched a major surprise offensive crossing the Niger River and attacked the western part of the country. They easily captured the city of Benin, Capitol of the Midwest, thus greatly increasing Biafran territory, but there was an inexplicable delay of one week before advancing further. Taking advantage of the delay, Federal forces hastily reorganized and set up strong defensive positions around Ore, one hundred and thirty-five miles East of the Federal Capitol city of Lagos. By the time the Biafrans reached Ore they were met by fierce resistance. The battles that raged in the following weeks resulted in the Biafran troops being compelled to retreat. By early October, 1967, they had fled back across the Niger River, and from that time forward, never posed a serious threat to the Federal Government.

With the defeat of the Biafran troops at Ore, the Ibo strategy gradually abandoned any hope of conquest of the Federal forces or control of a unified government or even a negotiated settlement based on a bifurcated North/South government. They, rather, could only hope for autonomy in the East and, finally, only struggled for the survival of the Ibo People itself.

This novel begins in July of 1969, when the Federal forces were massing for the final thrust into Biafra. This piece of fiction is set during those last months of that war and immediately thereafter. Although an attempt has been made in this work to accurately portray the timing and placing of events during that period, some dramatic license has been taken; the characters and their backgrounds are imaginary and are in no way intended to depict any actual persons, living or dead.

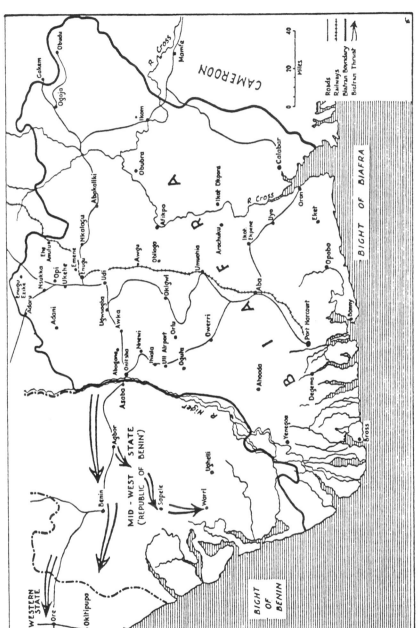

Map 3–1 • Biafra at the Height of Its Power, August 1967 (from John de St. Jorre, *The Nigerian Civil War*, p. 155)

CHAPTER 1

Between Iladan and Ilorin at the Frontier between the Western and Kwara States, Nigeria, July 5, 1969.

Paul brushed at the tiny flecks of black soot that clung to his moist arm. The ancient train had stopped dead on the long, curving hill. There was not even a slight breeze to relieve the hot stickiness of the crowded compartment and its fetid smell. He leaned out the window. The train's engine was hidden from his view on the curve ahead in the lush rain forest. He could see refugees with their loads perched precariously, sitting on tops of the old, wooden, British railway cars. Others were leaning out of open windows, shouting and gesticulating wildly. Still others had jumped down to relieve themselves near the tracks at the edge of the jungle.

"What is it? What's the trouble?" Paul called to one of the train guards passing below his window.

"No power," the guard shouted back. "The load is too great for the engine and the tracks are wet. The engine must take half of the train ahead to Ilorin and come back for us. Too many people - a thousand and one, a thousand and one," the guard whined, looking at Paul for reassurance and guidance. "What am I to do, what am I to do?"

"I don't know," Paul said, shrugging his shoulders.

The guard, bewildered and disappointed, walked on. Paul looked around his first-class compartment that was designed to hold four people comfortably but now held eight. Although he knew that he should consider himself fortunate to have gotten a seat at all, he felt in no way lucky. Instead he felt overwhelmed by lethargy and a sense of loss. After last night he wondered if anything mattered. It was a great effort to keep her from invading his mind. Knowing that he would punish her by never seeing her again, never calling or writing, never forgiving her, did nothing to diminish his sadness.

He glanced over at the boyish-looking American sleeping in the corner of the opposite bench, almost hidden from view by the open door of the compartment. Paul thought that he and the tired American were the only non-Africans on the train. He had seen no others.

Suddenly the door was slammed shut and kicked open again. A young, hulking Nigerian with a mean face filled the doorway. He was very black, and his hair stood high on his head. He wore tight-fitting black slacks, carefully pressed, shiny black shoes with pointed toes, and a British army officer's khaki shirt.

The other passengers, who had been talking in various dialects, ceased speaking when the man appeared. His eyes traveled over each passenger and finally settled on one small black man seated next to the young American. The stranger sat on the bench across from the black man and leaned forward to tap his leg.

"You are an Ibo," the stranger said in a surprisingly gentle tone.

The black man shook his head and looked away from the grinning stranger. The stranger wouldn't back off. He leaned further toward his suspect. Raising his voice, he spoke again. "I can always tell Ibos."

The black man shook his head violently and kept his eyes on Paul.

"I am with the CID," the stranger said, screaming the letters so that all in the compartment would realize his power. To Paul, he was just one of hundreds of self-styled policemen who had appeared since the war began, who relished the sudden authority the new regime had given them.

"I am wondering why you are in Nigeria," the officer continued. "I never see Ibos again."

The accused man noticed that the other people in the compartment were eyeing him, which made him even more nervous. His voice cracked when he spoke up. "I am going to the north, sir."

"There is no place in Nigeria for the Iboman!" The officer now was shouting loud enough to be heard in several cars.

The black man looked to the open door of the compartment. But he wouldn't be able to leave for the officer had him cornered and trembling.

"Why then," he ranted, "do the Iboman form his own country? You Ibos are bushmen!"

The officer's hysteria kept the passenger mute.

The young American, who woke up when the officer made his entrance, began to whistle a melody, one of those cloying commercial jingles that refuses to leave your memory. The CID man shot his stare from the black man to the corner where the young American sat with his eyes still closed. His whistling reminded Paul of Maureen. She liked to whistle sometimes.

3

"Why do you whistle?" the CID man wanted to know. His voice was still raised but he had control of himself again.

"Because I like to whistle," the young man answered, softly and curtly. He smiled coldly. Paul noticed that his eyes were sky blue. They, and his thick, straw-colored hair, were the most attractive features of his long, angular face.

"Do you know it is not proper to whistle in front of others, while they are talking?" The officer spoke softly now, hoping his mild manner would shame the whistler into silence. But the young man liked his melody and wouldn't stop.

"Other people may not want to hear your whistle," the officer said, raising his voice in a kind of shrill plea; he stood suddenly, moved toward the window and stared out, trying to compose himself.

Taking advantage of the distraction, the Ibo slipped through the open door. The CID man jumped to the door and shouted after the passenger in the Ibo dialect. In a moment he was back, glaring at the American.

"You are interfering with my duties. That man has gotten away. I can have you arrested at the next station," he threatened, again sensing his power. "This country is filled with foreign spies." Carefully, keeping his eyes on the American, the officer took a small black book from his shirt pocket.

"What is your name?" he demanded.

The American was not afraid to answer. "Larry Bartlett."

"Where is your passport?"

"In my bag," Bartlett said, pointing to the space above the seats which was stuffed with the passengers' baggage.

"You must carry your passport on your person at all times," the officer commanded.

4

Bartlett sat silent, returning the man's stare.

The officer parroted his favorite line. "I could have you arrested for not carrying your passport on your person." He paused to give extra power to his words, then barked another order. "Take down your bags and give me your passport."

While Bartlett obeyed his intimidator, Paul stood up and moved quickly toward the CID man, opening his wallet to expose the special green and white identification card that was granted normally only to senior field-grade officers and ministers of the country. He did not hesitate before speaking.

"I am a special representative of the minister of communications. I am on my way to the north."

"Yes, sir," the CID man said demurely, looking at the card. Paul immediately sensed his submissiveness and continued the power play.

"This man is my colleague," he said, raising his voice slightly for effect and pointing to Bartlett. "And that man who left the compartment is his steward. They are traveling with me to Kaduna to meet with the minister of communications on very important federal business."

Without looking away from the officer, Paul took a small note pad from his denim shirt pocket. After almost two years in the country he was familiar with the theatrics of petty civil servant officialdom. "What is your name?" he demanded.

"Joseph, sir."

"Joseph, you are annoying my friends. If you continue to do so, I will personally report you to the minister. Do you understand?"

"Yes, sir. I am very sorry, sir," the CID man said, bowing slightly. He passed Bartlett without a word and left the compartment. The next moment was filled with relieved sighs and grateful laughter.

"Thank you," Bartlett said, standing up and extending his hand to Paul. "You're an American?" he asked with an eager smile.

Paul returned the smile. "Yes, I am."

He motioned in the direction of the empty aisle outside the compartment and Bartlett followed him. They stood face to face in the narrow space before the window that opened onto the rain forest. The late afternoon sky had darkened and a breeze had started up, but still the train was stifling. Paul lit a cigarette, took a long, deep drag, and exhaled smoke as he spoke.

"Larry, how long have you been in country?"

"About three weeks," Larry answered, shifting his weight from his right leg to his left one; he could not stand still for very long.

Paul was not surprised by his answer. Larry obviously didn't understand the country.

"Let me give you some advice," he said. "For your own sake, don't interfere in these people's feuds. Their problems have been going on for many years before independence and there will continue to be problems for many more years. Don't get involved! You'll live longer."

Larry smiled ingenuously. "But that's why I'm here. I'm with EMMS," he said.

"Is that one of the small independents?"

Larry looked confused. "Independent what?" he asked.

"Oil companies."

Larry laughed suddenly and loudly. "Oh, God, no." he said, still laughing. "It has nothing to do with oil. EMMS stands for Evangelical Medical Missionary Society."

Now Paul looked surprised and felt a little stupid.

"Sorry," he said, hoping his face wouldn't stay red too long. "I knew it wasn't one of the Seven Sisters, but I thought it might be one of the little guys. Most Americans still living here are with oil companies." Paul was tapping the floor with his foot. "So, you're a missionary?"

6

Larry was quick to reply. "A medical missionary, right."

"What does that mean?"

"It means I'm also a physician. A medical missionary tries to meet the health needs as well as the spiritual needs of people wherever we are. Our headquarters are in Omaha, Nebraska, and we have small groups all over the world. I'm heading north to work at a new mission that's opening soon."

"All the more reason to keep a low profile," Paul said. He was interrupted by a clap of thunder that shook the railcar. Half a moment later, heavy drops of rain were slamming against the train, turning the landscape into a kaleidoscope of green and grey, and drumming on the tar roof. Paul felt his legs being cooled by a slight spray. "They're looking for missionaries now. All traveling foreigners are suspect, especially missionaries."

"But why?" Larry clearly didn't understand. Paul was slowly becoming weary of his ignorance.

"You obviously don't read the papers. Some of the so-called missionaries," he almost spit out the word, "have been aiding the Ibos in Biafra. You say you're going north. May I ask where?"

"Of course," Larry answered eagerly, implying that Paul did not have to ask quite so politely. "To the plateau."

Paul relaxed a little. "That, at least, is in your favor. But hold off on your proselytizing until you get there. You could have gotten yourself into real trouble with that guy."

Larry understood that Paul was concerned for his welfare. He was grateful and promised to act more sensibly.

"And thank you again, Paul, for bailing me out." He looked at Paul quietly for a moment, then turned to return to the compartment, but Paul stopped him with his comment.

"Don't thank me. I was protecting myself as well," he said. He flashed a smile then, just as quickly, was not smiling. "I know how these guys operate. He was feeling his way along. He was pushing, and unless he was pushed back, unless he met some resistance, he would have been at me, after you. You must remember that some of these guys have been told that they have the English to thank for all their problems. And maybe they do. But as a result, some of them hate *baturi* - us non-Africans. And with their new-found power, suddenly they can have revenge for the frustrations of their lifetime."

Paul began to whisper to accent his words. "But remember most of the poor dogs of this country, and even some of the truly powerful, still feel intimidated by non-Africans. And this feeling runs very deep. So, sometimes you just have to resort to the old colonial mentality. Sometimes it works, but it helps to have a pass from the minister to back you up."

Paul winked and laughed at his last remark because he realized that he was responsible for the somberness between them. Then he kept to more sociable inquiries.

"Where on the plateau will you be staying?"

Larry was glad for the easier question. "Our church runs a small school near Jos. That's where I'll be. My father has arranged for me to stay with an English doctor for a few weeks. Then I'd like to start my own clinic." He hesitated a moment to decide how much Paul would be interested in hearing. "I've just finished my internship at home. In our church everyone makes a commitment to serve two years, either at home or in the missions. I wanted to come here."

"You're very lucky! Life on the plateau is a delight, compared to other parts of the country. That's where I'm going, too. I have a house, it's not mine really, just outside Jos. You'll have to come to supper sometime."

The rain had slackened; other passengers had left their small compartments to take the air. Larry followed Paul back into their room.

"Jos is quite European. There isn't another city in West Africa like it," Paul said, sitting down on the cushioned bench seat across from Larry and relishing the temporary luxury of an almost empty compartment. The new freedom put him in an expansive mood.

"During colonial days it was the only place that held any attraction for Europeans who worked in West Africa. You know that West Africa was quite different from East and South Africa because there were very few Europeans settling here. East and South Africa had highlands, coffee plantations, temperate climates, and natural game reserves to lure Europeans; West Africa was called the white man's grave. The only people who came here were slave traders, explorers and missionaries. How's that for contrast? The slave traders and explorers were smart enough not to stay very long, but the missionaries came to live and they were usually dead within six months. But they kept coming. That's why the Ibos are so goddamned smart, and why they've got themselves into hell."

"How do you mean?" Larry felt he was fortunate to have met someone who could tell him about where he was going.

"Since the 1500s, missionaries have worked along the coastline, the Ibo and Yoruba territories. They penetrated as far inland as they could. They proselytized and they modernized, and the Ibos were quick to take it all in and learn as much as possible. As a result, the Ibos were practically running this country, prior to independence and the war."

"And the north?"

"Aye." Paul seemed to expect the question. He took a moment to plot his history lesson. "Did you ever hear of

9

a gentleman by the name of Uthman Dan Fodio and his jihad?"

Larry shook his head. He was embarrassed by his ignorance.

"You're forcing me to give you an abbreviated history course," Paul said professorially. "Uthman was the man who conquered the north in the name of Islam early in the last century. And I, as a child of technology, appreciate the fact that he conquered by using the horse."

Larry loved horses and was delighted to hear of their part in the conquest.

"It's true! His cavalry was the finest this continent has ever seen. The only problem was that they couldn't penetrate the rain forests of the south because of the tsetse fly. It killed off their horses. And the missionaries couldn't come up north because of Uthman's cavalry. So, stalemate - with part of the country modernized and the other part still feudal."

Paul wasn't used to lecturing. He needed a breather, so he lit another cigarette. Then he continued.

"And that's the way it stayed, until the British came. They introduced a system of indirect rule and were able to stay in power by playing on the divisive elements within the country: religion, ethnic groups, regional hatreds. And they brought the Ibos into the Civil Service because they were so effective."

Larry interrupted. "But they've been gone for years."

"Yes, gone but still remembered, in their language, their laws, their culture." Paul rested his head on the cushion behind him. "And the time bomb they left behind - that seems to be their style."

Larry looked as though he wanted to say something but he remained silent. Paul took a last drag on his cigarette.

"End of history lesson. You get a B+ for listening.

"This is the way it should be," Paul announced, lifting his feet to the cushion across from his seat. "It could be a pleasant trip."

Larry disagreed playfully. "It's not been so bad. I'm fascinated by this country. It's a new world to me."

"Wait 'till you get to Jos."

"Where is your home, Paul?"

"My house is in Washington, D.C., but my *home* is in Virginia. I work for an international telecommunications firm. I have been here for almost two years. I am based near Jos, and for the past two months I've been down near Port Harcourt." Paul's voice trailed off. He realized he might have revealed too much about himself.

But Larry had more questions. "How is it down there?"

"Disastrous. That region adjoins the large river delta area which now seems to be of strategic importance to both the federal government and the rebels. When I left, the federal forces were building up in Port Harcourt for a big drive into the Rivers area." Paul yawned and stretched his arms. "Quite apart from the war, I don't like the climate down there. I guess I'm basically a colonialist; I prefer cool, open grassland and mountains to mangrove." He grinned impishly.

"I thought the rebels," Larry said the word curiously, as if it might be a misnomer, "were all but finished."

"Everyone says they're finished," Paul said, "but I believe they're on the offensive in some places. They were still fighting hard when I was in Port Harcourt."

The train lurched suddenly, nearly throwing the two men to the floor. Evening air began to circulate through the compartment and Paul could smell the sweet perfume of the delicate frangipani flowers.

By the time the train reached Ilorin the next morning, they had left the lush rain forest, and as they traveled north, the landscape changed dramatically. The foliage became more sparse and trees were less plentiful, only dotting the open, brown savannah in small clusters. The trees of the north were of a different shape: against the open horizon they resembled umbrellas, flat on top with long, naked trunks.

By noon they had traveled through the grasslands and were into the scrub that was the last vegetation between the southern rain forest and the great northern desert.

Paul shifted his eyes from the sign on the carriage wall, warning travelers in the four main languages that they could die for smuggling arms, to the bone-white sand and brown, brittle scrub brush of the countryside. The frequency of the villages told him they were nearing Kaduna, capitol city of the north.

Paul and Larry jumped off the train before it had fully stopped in the teeming station. They pressed their way through the sprawling, sweating throng of traders, beggars, marketwomen, children and goats to the large taxi park at the gates of the station. Larry informed Paul he planned to take a lorry to Jos and Paul tried to dissuade him, explaining that only poor natives traveled by lorry. But Larry wouldn't change his mind, and Paul realized it would be futile to try, so instead he offered to share a taxi to the lorry park.

Paul bargained with the driver, who drove a hard deal, and they started through the sprawling federal city. New boxlike structures, immense and white, gleamed in the sunlight, competing for attention with the older, Islamic-style buildings and mosques. The taxi arrived across town just as the lorry was loading. Larry quickly climbed onto the old two-ton Mercedes Benz truck which had a wooden flatbed floor and a series of two-by-twelve parallel boards set across the bed between the high wooden walls. The lorry would transport him in neither style nor comfort, across the two hundred miles between Kaduna and Jos.

The taxi pulled away, Paul watched Larry sitting on his high bench, his blond hair and fair skin a startling contrast to the native passengers shouting encouragement at him and gesticulating madly at relatives on the ground who also had never seen a white man ride in a lorry.

Paul would never forget Larry's brilliant smile.

CHAPTER II

North Central State, Kaduna, Nigeria, July 8, 1969.

The evening sky was purple, laced with traces of red from the sun which had just set. Already Paul could see a star or two, or were they planets, he wondered, as he sat at the table near the edge of the large swimming pool. The luxury of the newly built Humdala Hotel, a palace of glass and steel in the center of Kaduna, was what he most needed after the twenty-four hours or so he'd spent on the train from Lagos. This was his first opportunity to relax in a long time. He would try to see the minister tomorrow. He would be surprised - Paul wasn't expected so soon. Then later in the week he would catch a flight to Jos and be back on the plateau where he longed to be.

The night desert air was cool and dry. He nursed a tall gin and tonic while looking at the placid water lit from below by blue-green lights. He was alone except for the bartender and a steward huddled together over the bar on the far side of the pool. He luxuriated in the thought that his suite beckoned a short elevator ride away. But he couldn't help himself; he began to relive that last night in Lagos. It had only been a few days ago when he was in Lagos. He still couldn't believe that it was over; that he had walked out on her. He would always remember that night as though he were experiencing it for the first time.

It had been nine o'clock on July 4th, an evening made delicious by a rare sea breeze that was driving away the hot, moist air over Lagos. He could see from the cars that jammed the driveway of the American Embassy a party was going on and the place would be sweating with people. Rows of Japanese lanterns, strung along the pillared porch and the tree-lined walk that led him from the driveway to the house, rocked gently in the sweet wind. He wondered how she would react to his surprise visit. He hadn't seen her for over a month, and the prospect of being with her again in a moment's time encouraged him to fairly dance his way to the embassy's front door.

He wasn't certain what he found so attractive about her. Maybe it was that there were so few expatriate women in the country then. No, he answered himself, that wasn't it. She was beautiful, and he knew that the competition for her attention would be keen. He had never had problems with women; they seemed almost naturally attracted to him. He was conscious of his dark good looks which gave him confidence with women. He never came on strong; understatement was his proven approach. Even the native women found him attractive, and it had never been difficult, wherever he was, to find someone eager to sleep with him.

But his approach was failing him with Maureen Cahill. He had known her for over six months and he had not yet been to bed with her. Tonight he would give her an ultimatum. Tonight he felt the need for her, especially after

15

what he had been through down in the Rivers area outside of Port Harcourt. It was odd that he had thought about her so often down there. Usually he never gave women a second thought.

A giant Hausa man guarded the entrance. A gracefully curved Maidugari knife in a colorfully beaded sheath dangled from the huge bicep of his left arm. His well-developed upper torso was naked except for a beaded leather vest. He wore dark trousers tucked into soft desert boots.

"*Sannu da aiki*," Paul said to the doorman, who reminded him of something out of the Arabian Nights.

"*To ranki titi*," the doorman replied, his face breaking into a huge grin. He bowed slightly, allowing Paul into the foyer, and shook his fist in the traditional Hausa greeting of respect. Paul felt complimented that he rated a *ranki titi* remembering that the salute was suitable for an emir.

The reception room was deserted giving Paul a chance to admire several priceless pieces from the Cahills' art collection. Small ebony Yoruba wood carvings contrasted subtly with two Marguerite Zorach paintings and a William Zorach sculpture. Coveting the sculpture, Paul passed through open French doors onto the patio, into the party.

The patio adjoined a large flower garden that was packed with expatriots in formal dress and the native elite resplendent in their long and colorful caftans and *regas*. Paul searched for a familiar face amid the sea of smiling, drinking revelers. He had never noticed it before, but all the expatriate women somehow looked the same, with their carefully coiffured hair and elegant evening gowns. The men in white dinner jackets looked restless. The natives, he thought, had it all over his compatriots, looking regal yet comfortable.

Paul felt out of place in his light blue tropical suit and decided to leave and come back in the morning. As he began to sneak away, he heard someone calling his name. He turned around to see who it might be.

"Paul!"

A red-faced, very American-looking man in a powder blue dinner jacket, with a full crop of white hair combed straight back from his tan forehead, was making his way through the crowd toward him.

"Mr. Ambassador!" Paul was delighted to see Maureen's father.

The diplomat arrived at Paul's side. He was sweating and wiped his brow with a white linen handkerchief. In his other hand he held a heavily iced drink.

"Good to see you, Paul! I didn't think you'd be back so soon," Mr. Cahill said, switching his handkerchief into the hand that held the drink, grabbing Paul's hand and shaking it vigorously.

"Got back a little early, sir," Paul said. He held the Ambassador's hand for a few seconds.

"What a mess - that whole area - nothing but trouble and suffering," the ambassador said, shaking his head and looking sincerely sad for a moment. Then he was smiling broadly. "How are you? God! You're looking great! Have a drink."

"No thanks, Mr. Cahill. I'll get one later."

"Christ, call me Joe! You're practically in the family," Mr. Cahill said, patting Paul on the back.

Paul got directly to the point of his visit. "Where is she?"

The ambassador stood on his tiptoes, straining to see over the heads of his guests. "Saw her not too long ago. Maybe she's up at the pool."

Paul felt obliged to explain his informal appearance. "I didn't know you were having a party, sir. I thought I'd surprise Maureen. I feel kind of out of place."

17

Mr. Cahill put Paul at immediate ease. "Nonsense!" he said. "After what you've been through? Anyway, this is just a welcoming party."

"Welcoming?"

"Yes, Paul, they're starting to come back, all the bloody Britons and Americans who fled when the first shots were fired just over two years ago. They're returning now and they're keeping me damn busy." The ambassador laughed and sipped his scotch. "You wouldn't believe the business opportunities, the oil and all. It's going to boom, now that the war's over!"

"Is it?" Paul asked, half hopefully, half cynically.

"Well, almost." The ambassador sounded convinced. "There are just a few rebels holding out down there now."

Paul was glancing around the patio; he wasn't paying attention to his host.

"How is she?"

Mr. Cahill answered with proper fatherly concern, "I think she wants to go home."

Paul nodded that he understood. "After two more months on the plateau, I'll be ready to leave myself."

"I think the war is really starting to depress her," Mr. Cahill said, looking again for his daughter.

Paul became excited by a new idea. "Maybe she would come back north with me, back to Hill Station! She was happy there once."

"Wonderful idea, Paul!" Mr. Cahill nearly shouted his approval and clasped Paul's hand. "Talk to her about it."

Now Paul couldn't contain himself. "I will. Where do you think she is?"

"Go on up to the pool, son. I'm sure she's up there. But you stop and see me and Mrs. Cahill before you leave, you hear?"

Paul promised that he would say goodnight later and left the ambassador to be cornered by a big, blond woman, wearing large diamond earrings, waving wildly and shouting, "There you are!"

Paul made his way quietly but quickly through the crowd toward the narrow path on the far side of the patio that wound up a little hill to the pool. The ubiquitous Japanese lanterns cast little light on the walk, and he often stumbled. As he neared the pool, he expected the sounds of splashing water and swimmers laughing, but he heard only the muffled sounds of the party below. More lanterns had been hung at the corners of the pool, sending out red and orange streaks across the still water.

Paul stood for a moment to let his eyes get used to the new darkness. He thought he could distinguish, at the far end of the pool, a lone figure sitting in a chair. He approached the silhouette.

"Maureen?" he whispered.

The only response was silence. He repeated her name as he neared the person in the chair. Then he saw it was not Maureen but a man.

"Who are you looking for?" the stranger whispered in a flat, low voice.

"Maureen Cahill."

"She's the daughter of the host, isn't she?"

Paul murmured, "yes."

"She's over there," the man said. He pointed to a small changing room at the far end of the pool.

"Oh, she's changing?"

"You her husband?" the man demanded.

"No, a friend," Paul said, turning to leave.

"She isn't alone, you know," the man said eagerly. Paul could tell from his voice that he was smiling.

Paul was not amused and snapped, "What do you mean?"

"I mean she isn't alone in there. A black man is with her." The man spoke softly and slurred many words. He had an English accent.

19

Paul suddenly felt sick in his gut. "It can't be true," he said, half to himself.

"Well, it is true," the man assured him. "I was sitting up here alone and I saw them come up the path and go in there; they didn't see me. I was going to leave but I was afraid they would come out before I got away. I don't fancy catching her in a compromising position."

"It must be someone else," Paul said, a trifle desperately. Then he remembered someone telling him that she had somehow changed recently. He tried to remember who it was that had said it. He couldn't remember, but he knew it was someone he thought a credible source. The person had said something about Maureen being very active with the Ibos. There was a hint that it was an embarrassment to the embassy. But he remembered he had dismissed it at the time as youthful idealism. Now things started to fit together.

"No, it's the ambassador's daughter. I saw her earlier at the party. I'm positive. She's very beautiful."

Paul felt helpless. What could he do? He couldn't bust in on them. He felt beaten and foolish and used. He wanted to run, but felt too weak. He returned halfway down the path, and waited.

After a short time, the strange Englishman passed him on his way back to the party. Paul, watching carefully, saw him stagger slightly for a moment. A surge of relief flooded Paul. The man was drunk, therefore he couldn't be trusted. Paul continued his vigil in a better frame of mind, though still not knowing quite what he would do when they came out.

He didn't have to wait much longer. A few minutes later he heard a door open and close, then voices whispering, then a splash and carefree giggling. It was Maureen's laughter. He started up the path and soon was passed by a strange Nigerian walking away from Maureen's laughter. Paul couldn't see him clearly and they didn't speak to one another. Paul stopped at the edge of the pool

20

and called out, "Maureen!" As he said her name, he heard in his voice joy and anger.

"Paul?" Her voice came from the water. "You're back! How wonderful! But I didn't expect you for another month."

"Got back early," Paul said. His voice was thick and sounded strange even to him.

"Come on in, the water's great," she called, and breast-stroked to the far end of the pool.

"I didn't bring a suit."

"There's one in the changing room."

He hurried into the room, snapped the light on, found the dark, damp nylon boxer-style suit hanging on a peg, stripped, put on the suit, ran to the pool and dived into the water. He swam to the far end of the pool where she was. She laughed and swam away from him, teasing him. He followed her to the middle of the pool and grabbed her arm, turning her around to face him. They stood with water up to their necks. He kissed her, kissed her hard, once, twice, three times. She gasped for breath, pulled out of his embrace and stepped backward. He leaped through the water to her and unfastened the large button that held her bikini top together. She moaned slightly but stepped farther away from him. But he wouldn't surrender; his hands cuddled her firm, well-shaped breasts. He pulled her body against his. She continued to resist, pulling him with her across the pool until her back was against the wall. There, then, he kissed her again and slipped his hand under her briefs.

She cried out softly, "Stop it!"

His fingers wouldn't stop caressing her, probing her.

"Paul, stop it!" she ordered again.

He took his hand away and let her go. She grabbed her bikini top, which was floating next to her, and turned her back to him to put it on. After she had climbed out of the pool, she stood at the edge looking down at him.

"Come on out, Paul." Her voice was cool and strained.

He didn't say anything, just stared up at her. He wanted to say, "You'd let him touch you, but not me," but he couldn't.

She managed a weak smile. "I'm going to change. I'll meet you down at the party." He realized that she had no idea that he knew what she had done.

When she left he turned into the water and swam fiercely to the far end. He wanted to exhaust himself. In smooth, coordinated strokes he began lapping the pool. After twelve rounds without stopping, he was exhausted. He got out of the pool, changed his clothes and walked down through the patio, through the party, and out of the embassy. As he walked, he repeated his vow not to see her again. He knew that he could not forgive her. The next day he would be on the first train to the plateau, the only place he wanted to be now.

CHAPTER III

Between Kaduna and Jos, Benue - Plateau State,
Nigeria, July 10, 1969.

Paul was seated on a long bench in the back of the
Volkswagen bus that was carrying many more people
than it could transport safely. He had never imagined
himself taking this kind of public transportation to Jos,
but it was his peculiar luck that no planes were flying to
the plateau because the weather there was miserably wet
and the forecast was not promising.

Paul knew that sometimes during the rainy season low-
flying clouds would catch and cling to the craggy rocks
on the plateau, cloaking everything in wet, grey fog.
There was a five-week period, unique in all of West Africa,
when the weather wouldn't change. Paul enjoyed it im-
mensely because it reminded him of the delights of a
North American winter. His house, and a number of others
on the plateau, had fireplaces, which he kept ablaze
this time of year.

In Kaduna Paul had missed seeing the minister who had
been unexpectedly called to Ibadan. So there was no

reason for Paul to stay on in Kaduna, despite the lack of fast, comfortable transportation to Jos.

At least this bus was preferable to the lorry that Larry had redden on out of Kaduna. It was enclosed, in case of rain. His back was flat against the metal partition that separated the driver from the passengers. He had been the first one on the bus at the crowded Kaduna station early that morning, but now he regretted his haste for he felt slightly claustrophobic. He kept reminding himself that he would soon be on the plateau.

Six people were seated to Paul's left; seven more faced him from the opposite bench. He had wondered, as he watched them boarding at the lorry park, how many people the driver would allow on before they started. He had put his bag under his bench because the aisle was blocked with the baggage of the other passengers. Paul could just see over their heads, out of the openings in the back door which was wired shut. A long, white dust chain trailed the bus.

It was late afternoon and they had been on the road for six hours, stopping at each village but only occasionally being able to get out. In the distance Paul could see the plateau, looming blue and grey and brilliant above the dry, white desert. A hot, parched, dust-filled wind rattled in through the tiny, rectangular openings that served as the bus windows, making Paul sweat and gag and think of her.

They had first seen each other on a road, which although improved, was not unlike the road he was traveling now. Then, he was leaving Lagos. The federal army had provided him with two jeeps, drivers and a temporary aide, Lt. Ndola. The second jeep was for security, because at night no one could guarantee the safety of any road and, with the curfew in effect, official travel was the only way to avoid problems at the dozens of federal checkpoints along the ninety miles of well-paved tarmac road to Ibadan. They had left the city at dusk. Paul had to be in Ibadan in the morning for an early meeting.

They had been on the highway about half an hour when they were stopped at the third roadblock. Even though they were in federal military vehicles, they were required to show their passes. The guards snapped a salute and immediately lifted the barrier, and as the jeeps began to move again, Paul noticed a white minibus stopped on the other side of the gate. Its passengers were lined up against the side of the bus. Two guards one with a flashlight, another with a rifle, appeared to be interrogating them. Each passenger had his bundles before him on the ground, open for inspection.

Paul spotted an attractive blond girl in the line. She looked so out of place standing there. He ordered his driver to pull over. Lt. Ndola, who was in the following jeep, came immediately to Paul.

"Trouble, sir?"

"What's happening to that group?" Paul asked, gesturing toward the minibus.

The young, Sandhurst-trained officer said he would investigate and approached the guard with the rifle. The guard, seeing him coming, set his gun down and snapped to attention with a salute and a loud "Sah!"

When the guard had finished his report, Lt. Ndola returned his salute and returned to Paul.

"He says they are looking for Ibos, sir."

"What about the *baturi*?" Paul asked, motioning toward the white woman.

Without a word, Lt. Ndola went back to the guard, who had his rifle trained on an old black man, while the other guard kept the flashlight on the man's face.

"Why is this woman to be interrogated?" the lieutenant demanded in English, pointing to the girl who was next in line. "Is she an Ibo?" he shouted.

"No, sir," the armed guard replied timidly. His shoulders drooped.

"Did you do this?" the young officer shouted, looking at the girl's belongings strewn around her feet.

"Yes, sir." The guard was losing his voice, while Lt. Ndola kept raising his.

"Why?"

"We are also looking for arms, sah."

"You suppose this woman is bringing arms?"

The young guard was afraid to look into Lt. Ndola's eyes.

"Put it back together," the lieutenant ordered.

The guard squatted and began gathering her things together. She bent down to help him. Paul called to Lt. Ndola from where he stood, bathed in the headlights of the jeep. He was wearing the uniform of an officer in the federal Nigerian army, a well cut dark green, freshly starched cotton fatigue jacket tucked into matching trousers. A webbed pistol belt, with the Seal of Nigeria as a buckel, hung around his thin waist, accentuating the trim line of his athletic body; on his head he wore a dark green, almost black beret without rank or insignia. The young officer was at his side instantly.

"Where is she going?" Paul was whispering to avoid being overheard.

"Back to Lagos, sir."

"Can we have the other jeep take her back?"

"We can. I don't think we'll need it, sir."

"I would appreciate it if you would take her back, Lt. Ndola," Paul said. "We'll be all right from here on."

She was still standing with the other passengers along the side of the bus, shielding her eyes from the jeep's lights. Paul wondered if she was as stunning face to face as she was from fifteen feet. Her blond hair was cut short, like a boy's, yet was totally feminine. Her breasts were full under her light colored blouse, and Paul wondered if her legs were really as shapely as they seemed in her handsome tan slacks.

He stopped studying her body when she dropped her hand from her eyes. Then she was watching him.

"I wonder what the hell she's doing here, but I don't have time to find out," Paul muttered to himself. Then he addressed Lt. Ndola. "I must be going. If you will be good enough to take her back to Lagos. With the curfew, there will be other roadblocks."

Lt. Ndola saluted smartly and left to escort the girl to his jeep. Paul took a last look at her, and for a moment he thought their eyes met. She was delightful to look at, he thought, but he had to admit that she was either a fool or a missionary; only one or the other would be on these roads at night. He gave her the benefit of his doubt and reckoned she was doing God's work. He was tempted to lose some time and lecture her on the dangers of traveling these roads but he figured it would do no good. He knew no one was more stubborn than a missionary.

Paul wondered, as his jeep pulled away from the roadblock, if she was an American. There were so few Americans still in country and most were fundamentalist missionaries. Paul had come to share the sentiments of many of his young African colleagues that the missionaries were do-gooders who bungled more often than they did any good; who had, in their zeal, contributed to colonial policies, and helped delay independence at least twenty-five years. Yet he wasn't entirely persuaded by his colleagues' arguments, because he knew that the missionaries had also brought education and modernization to the country, without which independence would never had come.

Still, he remained curious about the girl with the short hair and the long pants.

A sudden, chilly draft on his shoulders shook Paul from his reverie. The breeze now was much stronger and it came from the direction of the almost black clouds that covered the mountains ahead. Paul had noticed, as the road neared the plateau to begin its tortuous, six-thousand--foot climb, that the color of the earth had turned a rich red. When they began the ascent, it started to rain. It was not the hot rain of the south; now it was cold. Large, heavy drops pounded the red road and were immediately swallowed up in little explosions of dust. And as the rain fell still harder, it quickly turned the road a deeper, richer red until there was no more dust.

Not long after the rain began they reached the stretch of shiny black tarmac that led the rest of the way to Jos. The road wound still higher until it cut a final deep gorge in the red rock. Suddenly, the rolling, open, green meadows of the plateau spread before them. Paul could see cattle; it was one of the few places in West Africa where cattle grazed, free of the dreaded tsetse fly. He strained his neck to get a glimpse of the grasslands through the rain-streaked windshield. Dark clouds still hung low in the sky and the rain blew into the bus, onto Paul's shoulders, as the vehicle picked up speed on the straightening stretch of tarmac.

As they neared Jos, the rain lightened and finally stopped. An occasional ray of sunshine pierced the clouds, briefly bathing everything in a radiant glow. Paul admired the beautiful, well-kept gardens on the large expatriate compounds.

He was glad that Jos was built on hills; its narrow streets gave it a particular continental charm. They passed the large, modern Kingsway mini-supermarket in the heart of the European business district, following the narrow street lined with blooming jacaranda trees, their cerulean blue flowers reflecting a blue hue on the shiny tarmac and giving the whole street a fleeting, dreamy quality. The bus slowed as the streets became crowded nearer the sprawling, smelly market in the native quarter.

As they turned into the lorry park, the small bus was suddenly surrounded by at least two hundred people, all pressing themselves against the lurching vehicle. The driver pounded on the horn and cursed madly, and then gave up and stopped the bus just inside the gate. The faces that pressed against the window caused Paul to shudder. He recognized their look of terror, which he knew from the face of the Ibo man on the train.

As Paul groped under his seat for his bag, the bus became entirely dark, as if someone had thrown a heavy blanket around it. He looked up and could see nothing but legs and arms and heads squirming through the narrow windows. Everyone was shouting and screaming. The back door of the bus was still wired shut, yet people were fighting madly to get in. Paul turned to shout at the driver and saw that he had vanished.

Paul began to think that he would be crushed. He struggled to stand up in the swarming mass and suddenly found himself being pulled through the kicking and screaming and crying. He was being forced toward the closed doors and found himself fighting for air. The door burst open and Paul was thrown to the ground, surrounded by people still fighting to get on the bus. His legs were shaking and his nose was bleeding. He felt weak and wanted to just lie there but he knew that would be fatal.

He forced himself to stand up, retrieved his bag and ran, rubber-legged, to the park gate, where he hailed a taxi.

"Vom." Paul shouted the word at the driver.

The driver shouted back, "Three pounds."

29

Paul knew he was being robbed. It had only cost him ten bob to come all the way from Kaduna, but he was too tired and upset to bargain with the man. Vom was twenty miles north of the city.

"Trouble at the lorry park," Paul said as he climbed into the car.

"Iboman try to go to east, always trouble for Iboman," the driver said vindictively. "No place in Nigeria for Iboman!"

Paul sat in the back seat, trying to ignore the driver's comments and trying to relax as the car traversed the narrow streets of the city to the open road that led to the Bukuru. His compound was beyond the village, located on the enchanting arboretum-like grounds of the Trypanosomiasis Research Center.

Along the way, the taxi passed many large lorries heading for the city, each with a different name painted on the front: Honesty, Diversity, Juju Wine. Paul laughed at the signs. It hurt him to laugh, but he didn't mind the pain. Nothing could upset him now. At last he was back on the plateau.

CHAPTER IV

*The Jos Plateau, Benue-Plateau State, Nigeria,
November 10, 1969.*

The day was radiant, the azure sky cloudless. Paul guided his motorcycle along the narrow tarmac road that led from Bukuru to Jos. He rode past the large heaps of earth, small red mountains devoid of vegetation, the leavings of the tin mine, set next to the road. He passed an occasional expatriate compound nestled behind a large clump of trees off the road. He rode through the village of Bukuru, marked by a few one-story shops large open markets, and native bars. People, goats, dogs and chickens crossed in front of him, going from one market to the next.

When he reached the far side of the village, the green rolling hills of the plateau opened up before him. He sped toward a large clump of trees, silhouetted against the big sky about four miles ahead and off to the right. As he neared the place, he left the main road for the paved turn-off that led into an avenue lined by stately elms. A large sign read:

HILL STATION CLUB
STRICTLY PRIVATE
NON-MEMBERS KEEP OUT

As he neared the club he wondered why Larry wanted to see him. Paul had been back on the plateau four months and had met Larry by chance in Jos the week before while shopping. They were both in a hurry, but Larry had asked Paul if he could see him on an urgent matter. Paul suggested that they meet at his club for Sunday night dinner. The club was situated halfway between Vom and Jos, where Larry lived. The best meal of the week was served Sunday night when the few expatriates still living in the area gathered for dinner and then retired to one of the larger buildings of the compound to watch movies, usually old British comedies, a different one each week.

The density of the trees increased as Paul pulled the motorcycle into the widened space of tarmac where the road ended in a parking lot. On one side of the road was a row of small white, attached bungalows which had been used by expatriates coming into country or leaving. The cottages were now in a state of neglect. A high, white wall ran along the other side of the parking lot all the way to the squash courts at the far end. The whole place was shaded by a canopy of large evergreen trees at a doorway that had been cut in the middle of the wall. A native guard in a brown military-style uniform stood there.

"*Mun Godi*," Paul said.

"*Aliekam Salaam*," the guard responded as Paul passed through the doorway.

Inside the wall was a small courtyard where tables had been set up for dining *al fresco*. Carnations grew along the wall. The branches of tall fir trees hung over the wall, adding shade and quiet seclusion. Paul passed through the courtyard and entered the main door of the club which

which opened onto a large, dimly lit room. A long bar ran along the side of the room and curved into the wall at the end. The other side of the room held empty wooden booths. There was a small alcove with a circular dart board hanging on the wall. The floor of the room was highly polished, inlaid wood.

A good-looking young native, nattily dressed in a white tunic with silver buttons, his head topped by a red fez, stood behind the bar. "Good evening, sir."

"Good evening, Emmanuel."

Paul passed through the main building of the all but deserted club. He glanced into the dark, wood paneled snooker room which held two large, green snooker tables. A picture of the Queen, smiling benignly, looked down from one wall. In the small dining room Paul selected a table near the window so that they could look into the rear garden, now darkening in the evening shadows. He had agreed to meet Larry because he thought it would at least distract him from thinking about Maureen and perhaps, although he doubted it, help him to ignore the ache. Sometimes he knew he was being foolish; other times, he wondered if it really mattered.

It wouldn't be the first time that the two of them had acted as if nothing had happened. That had been their act when they met the second time, on a hot Lagos afternoon, two weeks after Paul discovered her on the road. He had just ordered a beer from his table on the deck overlooking the immense oval swimming pool at the Federal Palace Hotel where he was staying. He couldn't help but notice the couple lounging on the other side of the pool. They were the only twosome basking under the sun; everyone else was, like Paul, alone. Even from this distance, he thought the attractive girl in the pink bikini looked familiar. He knew that he had never seen her companion, a rather distinguished looking older man.

Just as Paul sipped the last of his beer, the man swan-dived into the pool and began taking slow laps. Paul saw his chance and approached the girl, reading in the shade of an umbrella. He planned to keep walking if he discovered, on closer view, that he had never seen her before. But he had.

"Excuse me," he said, flashing his most dazzling smile, "there is no way this won't sound like a come-on, but I think I know you."

She looked up from her book and removed her dark glasses. He knew then that she was the girl. She hesitated before replying, and Paul could tell from her quizzical expression that she was trying to recall his face. Then she smiled, shyly at first, then more openly. She did remember him.

Paul sat next to her. "Did you get back all right that night?"

"Yes. I wanted to thank you but I didn't know how to get in touch with you. I didn't know who you were." She spoke softly, and for some reason her voice made Paul notice her delicate, long-fingered hands. "I still don't."

Paul was delighted that she cared to know, and he introduced himself immediately. "My name is Paul Jeffries, and I think you're lovely."

She was clearly embarrassed and excited by his compliment. "I'm Maureen Cahill. My father," she gestured toward the man in the pool, "is the American Ambassador here," she said, extending her hand to him and smiling.

Paul held her hand for a moment and he wanted never to let go, but he saw that her father had left the water and was toweling himself dry. Paul relinquished her hand.

"I'd like you to meet my father," she said brightly, breaking the still silence.

Paul didn't want to meet anyone just then; he wanted to be alone with her, but she insisted.

"And I'd appreciate it if you wouldn't say anything about the circumstances of our first meeting, please." She seemed to be pleading with him, and for a moment her face was pinched and too white. Only later would Paul understand why.

"I won't, on one condition." He wanted to tease her.

She couldn't have guessed. "What's that?"

"That you go out with me tonight."

She smiled, her lips sliding back and open gracefully, showing all her teeth. Of all her smiles, it was this one Paul would remember most often.

"Hello, Paul!"

Paul looked up from his reflection in the windowpane to see the American missionary he had met on the train.

"Larry!" Paul got up promptly and they shook hands. "Please, sit down." He motioned toward the chair across from him. "Have any trouble getting in?"

"No. I just told them I was with you." Larry smiled. Paul handed him a menu.

"I recommend the roast beef and Yorkshire pudding."

"Sounds fine," Larry said, putting down the menu without reading it.

"Some wine?"

"No thanks, but please don't let me stop you."

Paul winked at him. "You won't. How are things with Dr. Stewart?"

"I've moved out."

"Why?" Paul was astonished. "How could you leave that lovely compound? Steward must have one of the most exquisite houses in Jos, with one of the best views."

"I wanted to be on my own," Larry replied, almost defensively. "I needed to be on my own. I guess it just wasn't my kind of practice."

It was obvious to Paul that Larry did not want to pursue the subject. But that didn't stop him.

"Where did you move to, Larry?"

"Sabon Gari."

"The native quarter?" Paul was a little surprised.

"Yes. I prefer it there. I've found a nice place."

"You and Stewart have a rift?"

"No. I didn't care enough about the practice." Larry paused, then added, almost as an afterthought, "You know, he only takes expatriates as patients."

Paul knew. "Was that the reason you moved out?" he asked.

"Part of it."

"What are the other parts of it, Larry?"

Larry understood that Paul was asking out of genuine concern, nevertheless he was irritated by his persistent questions. "I'd rather not talk about it," he snapped.

During a long silence, Larry studied the lighted garden. Then he seemed to relax.

"Speaking of Stewart," Paul said then, "I thought I saw him the other day with his Great Danes. One of them had a splint on its hind leg."

"Hit by a truck," Larry mumbled, still looking away from Paul.

"Sorry to hear that. I know Stewart adores those dogs. He takes them everywhere. He even brings them here." Paul laughed but he couldn't get Larry to join him.

"We spent six hours in surgery working on that dog, inserting a surgical pin," Larry said angrily.

Paul tried to calm him down. "It looked to me like the operation was a success," he said.

"It was."

"Then what's the problem? Why are you upset?"

Larry spat his answer. "Because we spent six hours operating on that dog, and then when we go in to Jos

36

we're surrounded by the most pitiable group of beggars and leper children, some in desperate need of medical care, and Stewart won't so much as give them sixpence, let alone tend to their medical needs! They don't exist for him." He slammed his fork on the table.

Now Paul was becoming agitated. He thought Larry was being too hasty in his judgment. "But he has a policy of only taking expatriates as patients," he said.

"What does that mean?" Larry demanded. "The need is there, in the village."

Paul couldn't defend Steward; he didn't know him well enough.

"Do you know what they call those children?" he asked.

Larry shook his head.

"Allah's pickin'."

Larry wasn't listening.

"I just can't believe that those children aren't hospitalized," he said. "Some of them are terminal. Yesterday I saw a boy who couldn't have been more than nine years old; his left foot and right arm were gone from leprosy, and he was hobbling with a homemade crutch around the Kingsway parking lot, begging."

Paul asked what Larry had done for the boy.

"I gave him a shilling."

"That's why they call them Allah's pickin'," Paul said.

Now Larry was listening. "What do you mean?"

Paul was happy to tell him. "Simply that begging is encouraged here in the north. There are no institutions for people like that, partly because in giving alms the giver has an opportunity to atone for his sins to Allah. It's a form of expiation."

Larry was still disgusted. "It's inhuman," he said. "And it's why I wanted to see you."

Paul was curious. "Why me? "What can I do for you?"

Larry wasted no time telling him. "I want to start a clinic here for these children. I've been thinking about it for a long time. But in checking around, I've run into nothing but brick walls. I know now the only way I can do it is with the help of the government here. Unfortunately, I don't know any officials. I travelled to Kaduna to see the minister of health, but he wouldn't see me. I know you have some contacts in Kaduna. Will you help me?" Larry was looking directly into Paul's eyes.

Paul was quiet, but Larry couldn't stop talking. 'I've even got a site picked out," he said.

Paul was surprised by this announcement, by Larry's passionate determination. He admired it.

"There's an old deserted club at Barakin Ladi, about forty miles from Jos."

"I know the place," Paul said.

"It wouldn't take much to fix it up," Larry said, and Paul was certain that Larry had investigated the site coutless times.

"Well, you're right about one thing," Paul said.

"What's that?" Larry asked, though he knew the answer.

"You can't do anything without government support. But, Larry, you don't think they're going to give that land away, do you?"

Larry anticipated the question. He had his answer ready. "No, I'm not that naive," he said. "I don't know if I've told you, Paul, but my father is coming over to join me, along with my brother and sister. Dad's retiring in June. He wants to help out with his pension. We could buy the land with that money. It would be a perfect place." Larry's body trembled with his excitement. Paul hated to deflate his enthusiasm, but he knew he must be realistic.

"It's not so much a question of buying the land," Paul said, "it's a question of *dash*."

38

Larry was not familiar with the word. "Dash?"

"Whom to pay off and how much," Paul said. He paused to drink from the mug of beer that the steward had brought him. "About the only help I could give you would be to try to find out who and how much. Finding the right person is critical. And I will try, but I'll tell you something: I don't think your father's pension would quite cover the bill."

Larry shrugged away the remark. "I know we can work out the money matters," he said. "Once we get the land, I can get most of the equipment we'll need from the States. Donations. I just need help in getting the land." He sighed and looked far away. "It's very beautiful out there. I don't know what it is; there's something so clean about it."

"You know, Larry, you're not only an idealist, you're a romanticist."

"Perhaps," Larry said. "But is there any other way to go through life?"

Paul could have answered the question, but he knew the reply was too depressing.

"You've got another problem to consider," he said, "and that's the fact that this is an Islamic society and things are done a certain way here. You can't expect to come here and suddenly start showing these people what you think is the error of their ways. They have been under colonial rule practically since the beginning of this century. They won their fight for independence, and they will not turn it over again to the white man. They've been there. They're suspicious of the motives of expatriots, and why should they help Christians?" Paul's deliberately cold tone sobered Larry. He was paying strict attention now.

"Nothing personal, Larry, but I myself don't happen to agree with what many missionaries have done and are still doing here."

Larry was silent for a moment. His face expressed hurt and surprise, as though Paul had struck him. "I don't know what to say," he replied. "Are you telling me that you won't help me?"

Paul knew he had to explain himself. "I know that all missionaries aren't rotten," he said, and Larry returned his smile. "And I already told you," Paul affected a spanking tone, "that I *would* help you!"

He got serious again. "I'm planning to go the Kaduna next month. I'll bring the matter to the minister's attention then. But he's the minister of communications. I can't be optimistic that he can help you."

Larry looked crushed. "Next month might as well be next year," he said quietly. "Some of those kids won't last a month. And with the weather so miserable, that dry, dusty wind. What do they call it?"

"The *harmattan.*" Paul respected Larry's feelings. "I'm sorry, Larry, that's the best I can do."

Larry understood, but was still despondent. "I know I can't stay here, watching those kids suffer, doing nothing. I'll leave the country first."

"Why don't you go back to work with Dr. Stewart? His patients need help, too."

"I can't do that," Larry said curtly. "You don't understand."

Paul shrugged his shoulders.

Larry, saying he wasn't hungry, shook Paul's hand and, slightly stoop-shouldered, walked away.

CHAPTER V

Kaduna, North Central State, Nigeria,
December 8, 1969.

Next month came quickly. The briefing had been set
for two-thirty on what turned into a blazing afternoon.
The minister had been very specific: he would meet Paul
at the Kaduna airport at ten that morning. His limousine
was waiting outside the modern terminal building. The
desert capital of the northern states was still a vibrant,
young city of modern glass and steel skyscrapers; a kind of
Calgary of West Africa, but instead of the Rockies, graceful golden-domed mosques highlighted the scenery. Paul
had been back on the plateau five months when he was
summoned to Kaduna, and he had just stepped off the
plane when a blast of hot, brittle air made him yearn to
return immediately.

David Kpamba was the youngest man in his country's
history to be minister of communications. He was thirty-
two, athletic, very handsome, cocoa-colored, with classic
Negroid features. He was standing beside his car when
Paul arrived, dressed in his native costume, a flowing

rega, which enhanced his appearance of dignity and gracefulness. Paul was genuinely pleased to see his friend again. He had been impressed with Kpamba since their first meeting a year before, when David had proposed a complete national telecommunications network plan. They had other things in common: they were the same age, they shared an interest in athletics, and both were electrical engineers.

Paul had one tremendous advantage over other telecommunications consultants in his relationship with the minister: he was an American. Kpamba had been educated in England and he left that country feeling both a grudging respect and a profound bitterness for the British. He felt no such antagonism for Americans however, and had always been impressed with their technological skills.

"Why the rush?" Paul asked as he sank back in the speeding, air-conditioned Chevrolet. "The meeting doesn't start until mid-afternoon."

Kpamba's face looked pinched and drawn. "I wanted to talk to you before the meeting, Paul," he said softly. "But first tell me where you will be staying."

"At the Hilton."

The minister instructed his chauffeur to drive to the hotel, then relaxed and addressed Paul confidentially.

"You should know that General Tarka Bello will be at the briefing."

The news surprised Paul but did not worry him, as the minister had expected.

"I thought he was too busy planning the final strategy of the federal army," Paul said.

Kpamba nodded his head vigorously. "He is preoccupied with the war, so the fact that he's going to be there indicates the importance that the government is giving to this meeting. They obviously know that they must buy off on the plan."

42

Paul thought a moment, then smiled at his friend.

"And if not," he said, "they'll soon be looking for a new minister of communications."

Kpamba was not in a joking mood. "Perhaps," he said seriously, "but that's likely to happen only if there's another coup."

The remark wiped the smile from Paul's face.

"Do you expect one?"

Kpamba shrugged his shoulders.

"In Nigeria, no one can say," he responded, gazing out at the wide, palm tree-lined streets of the city. "Maybe someday a sense of nationalism will replace ethnic loyalties. But I do not see that happening in the near future."

Paul was becoming anxious for his friend.

"But if a coup does come, what about you?" he demanded.

Kpamba turned to Paul and smiled easily. "Relax, my friend," he said with exasperating calm. "This country has had two bloody coups since independence, and not one minister of communications has been assassinated." He had a deep, melodious voice, a natural way of pausing for emphasis, and a good sense of the dramatic. "I just want to have enough money saved so that if I have to flee the country, I will have something to live on while in exile."

Paul said that was understandable and asked Kpamba if he would go to London to live.

"Perhaps," he answered tentatively. "Maybe even Washington."

Paul laughed aloud, delighted with the prospect. Then Kpamba changed the subject abruptly, handing Paul a letter. "I received this from the contractor yesterday. They are offering us a *deal*," Kpamba said the last word in an exaggerated American accent. "It seems good, at least on initial examination. You remember your telling me

about the desirability of putting a sixth earth station somewhere near Uli?"

Paul nodded.

"Well, if we can decide now to proceed with the Uli
earth station, we can make substantial savings for the
government," Kpamba said.

"But that's impossible!" Paul shook his head as he
spoke. "Don't they know that the proposed site is in the
middle of rebel territory?"

"They know, but maybe there is a way," Kpamba
said. He tapped Paul's shoulder when he saw Paul was
about to speak. "Please let me finish. The contractors
point out in their proposal that, given the economies of
scale involved in constructing the five earth stations already ordered, they can build a sixth at substantial savings
if they can get the go-ahead soon on procurement of the
sixth station.

"If, on the other hand, they have to wait six months or
a year for the government to approve a sixth station, the
various series of production line procurement will be
committed to produce only the five. And a new order for
a single earth station would result in having the whole
production process started all over again, with greatly
increased additional charges."

The limousine pulled up in front of the hotel as Kpamba
finished talking.

Paul spoke quickly, before Kpamba stopped him again.
"I agree, but there's one problem," he said. "We haven't
chosen a site at Uli. We've talked about some promising
possibilities, but before we can issue a go-ahead, we've
got to be sure that it's possible to put a station down
there."

Kpamba looked pleased, as though he had anticipated
Paul's statement. "That's why I wanted to see you this
morning," he said, as the hotel doorman opened the car

door. "I have a plan that I think will solve our problem and I want to talk with you about it before the meeting."

Paul said he would be happy to discuss the plan later.

"There's something I wanted to ask you, David," he added, waving the doorman off momentarily. "It'll only take a minute."

Kpamba waited for Paul to continue.

"There's a young man, an American, in Jos, a missionary," Paul began.

Kpamba raised his eyebrows slightly. Paul was getting nervous; he felt Larry's zeal.

"Well, he's also a physician, a medical missionary. He wants to start a clinic for lepers in Jos." Paul didn't know if he still had Kpamba's attention, but he proceeded nevertheless. "There seems to be an epidemic of leprosy there. Even I've noticed it. A lot of kids are stricken with it, too. Something should be done for them."

Kpamba remained silent, which encouraged Paul.

"This missionary knows about an old deserted club near Barakin Ladi. He wants to acquire the land and buildings for his clinic."

Finally Kpamba spoke. "And what's your interest in this matter, Paul?"

"I have no interest," Paul was quick to say. "I told him that I would ask around for him. He doesn't know anyone in the ministry. He tried to see the minister of health, but the minister wouldn't see him."

Kpamba laughed, and his laugh was tinged with cynicism. "I shouldn't wonder," he said. "Mohamed Abda isn't the most accommodating person in the world, particularly to Christian missionaries . . . "

Paul interrupted Kpamba to remind him that he had promised to ask about the land.

"You're sure you don't have any particular interest?" he asked, eyeing Paul with mock suspicion.

"What interest would I have?" Paul was becoming annoyed with the question. His voice reflected his anger. "You know I'm not particularly concerned about either religion or medicine."

Kpamba, realizing that Paul was serious, also became serious. "Where is the land again?" he asked in his most official voice.

"Barakin Ladi."

"In Hausa, it means 'the camp of the woman'," Kpamba said, looking Paul in the eye. "I will check with Abda."

The minister paused for a moment, then his voice assumed a delicate tone. He was sorry that he had to ask.

"How does your friend propose to pay for this land?"

Paul shook his head. He had expected the question. "That's going to be a problem," he said. "He told me that his father will contribute his pension to the clinic."

"Very irregular," Kpamba muttered.

"For Christ's sake, David," Paul said sharply, "the guy's a missionary! He doesn't have any money!"

"Relax, Paul, please," Kpamba shot back. "You know Abda would expect adequate remuneration. That land must be very valuable, like all land on the plateau. I think there are plans to make it a tourist spot after the war. And you should realize that there might be some political risk in helping Christian missionaries just now."

Paul had no more to say. He regretted that the subject had caused friction between them. After all, he didn't care if the clinic got started or not.

"I will check for you, Paul," Kpamba said quietly embarrassed. Then he smiled broadly, indicating a truce, and offered his hand to help Paul from the car.

The two men, harmony restored between them, entered the lobby of the new hotel.

Paul's slide lecture on future telecommunications de-development was over. The young minister stood up just as the lights went on.

"I'm sure that some of you have questions regarding Mr. Jeffries's overview, and he will be happy to answer them. But before that, I would like to add some information that has just come to my attention and that may affect any decisions made today," David said. He turned to Paul who made a gesture as though to indicate "after you" and sat down.

"As Mr. Jeffries has pointed out, standard earth stations are planned for the five major cities. We have been examining a number of sites for a sixth station." David motioned for the lights to be dimmed and another map, was projected on the screen. "One of the most promising sites happens to be here." He pointed to a large red dot on the map. "It's near Uli, which now, of course, is part of Biafra.

"As you know, Mr. Jeffries has just returned from an extended stay near Port Harcourt, examining that area for the earth station that we hope will be built there, in 1975. I feel that I cannot over emphasize the need for these earth stations. For the first time in our history, they will not only provide us with communication with other parts of the world previously inaccessible, but they will also give us access to our African neighbors, an access that we have not had heretofore in many cases, and one that we have never had directly.

"Perhaps the dream of pan-Africanism will at last be possible through this new technology." The minister's words were interrupted by statements of approval from the table.

"Mr. Jeffries has pointed out to me why locating an earth station near Uli would be ideal. First, as you can see from the map, a series of microwave towers extend from the general vicinity of the airport. These towers were built a number of years ago to link the offshore oil rigs to both Port Harcourt and Lagos. Moreover, these towers generally connect with the infrastructure of both the eastern and western regions' existing telecommunications networks" David jabbed at the map with the pointer as he spoke.

"Another reason why Mr. Jeffries and I believe that Uli would be an ideal site for the sixth earth station is that the equipment needed to build the station here could easily be brought in by both ship and plane. In many other cases, we will have to contract for extensive road building before we can begin work on the stations.

"Because this site is so easily reached by air and because there is now one large road already in existence, this location is clearly very desirable." The lights went on and the drapes were drawn to let the sunlight into the air-conditioned room.

"We are faced with a problem," David continued. "As you all know, the war cannot go on for much longer. Biafra is finished. But still the Ibos will not surrender. Unfortunately, we must decide soon – within a month, to be precise – whether we will build the sixth earth station near Uli. I have received a letter from our hardware contractors," he went on, picking the letter up from the table, "which informs me that in order for the necessary lead time for procurement, the contract for the sixth earth station must be signed by the middle of next month." He laid the letter back down on the table.

"This means that we have only three weeks to make our decision. But I do not feel that we can make an intelligent decision based on the evidence before us now. What we need is for someone to go to Uli, examine the potential, and return with the information so that we can make our decision. Only an expert can do this type of analysis, which, of course, will not be without its dangers."

David made a gesture with his hand toward Paul. "I have discussed this with Mr. Jeffries and he has informed me that he would be willing to undertake this endeavor, which I would never ask him to do unless I could assure him that he would be recompensed adequately for the rather extraordinary risks involved."

"Mr. Minister," General Bello said, "I have a question." The general spoke slowly, like a man groping for the right words. He was a Birom and had not been sent abroad for schooling, but what he lacked in refinement he made up for in a peasantlike common sense combined with a certain genius for military strategy. "Even if we could reach an arrangement with Mr. Jeffries to go to Uli, how could we arrange his transportation into that territory?"

"Sir, that is a good question! The answer is that we would provide for his transportation to the island of Fernando Poo, and from there he would take one of the relief planes that fly into Uli on a fairly regular basis." The general nodded his head in approval.

"Gentlemen, the savings to the treasury will be substantial. The sixth earth station would greatly add to our communications network. I leave the decision with you."

CHAPTER VI

Vom, Benue-Plateau State, Nigeria,
December 15, 1969.

Paul stood on the pillared porch of his two-story house in the long-shadowed silence of late afternoon, looking beyond the line of eucalyptus trees separating his compound from the large grassy meadow. He was watching a thin, tall boy, dressed in one piece of beige cloth and carrying a staff, herd twenty long-horned white-grey Fulani cattle across the meadow. The animals reminded Paul of the Brahman bulls used at rodeos in the States.

The boy wore his garment regally, with one bony shoulder exposed; the fabric, which resembled the color of his cattle, hanging to his knees like a cassock. He spotted Paul, stopped and stared at him for a moment, then waved his arm in a quick, birklike motion. Paul waved back immediately, and the boy urged his cattle to move on. Paul looked after them until he could no longer see the white egrets that followed them.

He was always glad to be back on the plateau. Another week had passed since the briefing in Kaduna and he was really starting to settle in. Only on the plateau did he feel secure, at rest, at home. He knew this peacefulness arose from the Islamic influence of the northern region which had infiltrated the plateau in recent years, instilling in the people a lasting conservatism. There was less progress here, but there was order, and Paul preferred order. He had only to consider what progress had done for the Ibos, who were now fighting for life, to know he didn't want the plateau to change like that.

The cold harmattan wind was blowing in from the north, filling the air with tiny dust particles that turned the sky a dark brown, filtering the sunlight to give the earth a yellow-orange tinge. It had not rained again since Paul first returned to the plateau six months earlier. That rain had come early, and everyone knew it was a freak because the rain birds had not come. The rainy season would not officially begin until the large, black birds arrived.

This was the time of the year that the Fulanis and other northern tribes hated most, for the harmattan blew unceasingly. Traditionally, it was considered the evil time of year, a time of disease and famine. Only rain would bring relief.

For Paul, the harmattan was only an annoyance. He had much to be grateful for. The plateau had given him a tranquility he had thought was lost to him, since he had known Maureen. When he had first come to live there it was difficult because he was alone and knew no one. His work absorbed most of his time, offering a welcome distraction. Occasionally he would have supper at the Hill Station Club, and he used the swimming pool there almost every day. He had met a few English expatriates at the club, but had little to do with them away from it. He spent most of his time working in the house that the minister had provided him.

Strangely, and for the first time, standing on the porch, Paul felt detached from anyone and everything, and he found the sensation not altogether unpleasant.

So much had happened in the past few months, that it was hard for Paul to believe that Maureen had actually come here. They had know each other for only a short time when he invited her to visit the plateau. Coincidence aided their plans: her father was planning a tour of the cities in the north, and she suggested to him that he begin his trip in Jos. They stayed at Hill Station, and each day Paul drove to the city to take them sightseeing.

It was a strange and fleeting visit. Maureen had stayed only five days, but they were among the happiest days of Paul's life. Their time together had been quiet, filled with long walks through his eucalyptus shaded compound; motorcycle trips to the mountains at the edge of the plateau, where they could look down onto the vast expanse of desert below, a scorching yellow wasteland; afternoon swims; and strolls through the fantastic gardens of Hill Station. It was only when they traveled into the city, where a few Ibo refugees could be seen, that she seemed distressed and preoccupied. He remembered telling her that there was nothing anyone could do for them.

For their last night together, he took her to a native bar in Jos. He remembered the place vividly: a large cement patio ringed by a cluster of buildings open to the stars. Paul and Maureen at a table that bordered the dance floor, drank palm wine as a very talented band played the rhythmic West African highlife music.

Paul watched the dancers flow with the music. The band began slowly, with subtle rhythms, and the dancers moved almost imperceptibly, movements that seemed so natural. Then, as the rhythm changed, the dancers came together, separated, and came together again. The dance became an erotic ritual between a man and a woman, bending over, thrusting pelvises, but all done gracefully to the music. It seemed so natural, so innocent.

Paul was caught up in it and, looking across at Maureen, he could see she was fascinated too. Awed by the graceful, sensual movements of the dancers, they danced too, knowing they were clumsy by comparison. But the music was hypnotic and they didn't care. They held each other close. He fell in love with her that night. And the next day Maureen was gone.

A large green van, bearing a USAID shield on the door, pulled into the circular driveway that ringed the flower garden in front of Paul's house, startling Paul out of his memories. An athletic-looking young man, wearing dungarees and a canary yellow shirt, jumped out of the van and leaped onto the porch.

"Hello," the man said, extending his hand to Paul. "I'm George Dodson from the consulate in Kaduna. You're Paul Jeffries, aren't you?"

Paul nodded, surprised, and mumbled, "Nice to see you." They shook hands and Paul spoke up, remembering his manners. "Please come in. How did you know I was here?"

Dodson smiled slyly. "We like to keep track of Americans, especially now," he said, following Paul into the sparsely but comfortably furnished main room. The floor was covered by a large Persian rug. Two easy chairs were strategically placed to take advantage of the view through the windows, and inexpensive pieces of African sculpture adorned the room.

"Make yourself at home." Paul said. "Tea?"

Dodson commandeered a chair that gave him a splendid view of the distant hills.

"Have any coffee?" the consul asked hopefully.

53

Paul said there was coffee somewhere in the house and called his servant. A young Birom, shiny black and dressed in a white, freshly pressed, military-style tunic with a mandarin collar and brass buttons, white trousers, and no shoes, hurried into the room.

"Ali, please fix tea for me and coffee for this master."

Ali nodded and in an instant he was gone.

"That's some outfit your steward's wearing," Dodson remarked.

"He came with the house," Paul said. "I guess the people who gave him to me think I'm a colonial."

"He's a dandy," Dodson said, smiling grandly.

Paul agreed whole-heartedly, then resumed playing host. "You'll stay for chop tonight, I hope," he invited heartily.

His guest answered tentatively, "I was planning to eat at the catering rest house."

Paul pretended to be offended. "Nonsense!" he protested. "Save yourself a couple of quid and eat here. Really, I'd enjoy your company. I haven't had much lately."

Dodson said he'd be honored and happy to eat with Paul.

Ali brought in a tray laden with cups, saucers, milk and sugar servers.

"Two masters for chop tonight, Ali," Paul announced.

"Yes, sir," Ali replied, bowing and holding the tray in front of Dodson. Then he served Paul, placed the tray on the table between the men, and returned to the kitchen to prepare dinner.

It was dark now. The brief African twilight was but a dim glow of a thin red line against the black outline of the faraway hills.

"How long have you been back from Port Harcourt, Paul?" Dodson asked, savoring the aroma of his coffee.

"About two months," Paul said. "Say, you have been keeping track!"

Dodson looked puzzled.

"I mean you knew that I was down there," Paul explained. "I came back just as I thought the rainy season was starting here. The sky was covered with clouds, cold and misty. It was such a relief from the Port Harcourt area, and such a delightful change. I don't ever want to leave this place. I guess it reminds me of home.

"Did you ever see a house in Nigeria with a fireplace?" Paul pointed to the stone fireplace in the center of the room. "But the rain lasted only one week and now the harmattan is pretty bad."

"It's cold," George said.

"That keeps the chill off," Paul said, meaning the blazing fire. The men watched sparks battle each other for air.

Dodson interrupted the silent watch. "From the plateau, you'd never know there was a war going on in this country," he said.

"I'd almost forgotten," Paul said wistfully, sipping his tea. "I don't like to think about it. I only hope it will be over soon."

"It won't last much longer. The Ibos are almost finished." Dodson spoke knowingly. Paul figured he must have official information, so he believed him.

"What a waste," Paul said. "They were such an advanced people."

Dodson placed his cup on the table and cleared his throat before speaking. "Paul, we have a problem, and I feel that you may be able to help us," he said.

"What have I done?" Paul was kidding, and he laughed, but he thought it sounded important.

"It's serious, I'm afraid," Dodson said.

Paul watched him pick up his briefcase from the floor by his chair.

"I'd like to show you something." Dodson pulled out a copy of a newspaper article and handed it to Paul.

AMBASSADOR'S DAUGHTER IN BIAFRA
by
Jim Garepy
Port Harcourt, Nigeria, November 20, 1969.

Twelve hours by pirogue from Uli through a juju-ridden area of mangrove swamp and a maze of creeks in the heart of rebellious Biafra, the daughter of the former American Ambassador to Nigeria, Joseph Cahill, is running a one-woman clinic on the tiny island of Bugamu to help starving Ibo children.

Maureen Cahill, 22, has been working in rebellious Biafra for one month. The idea for the clinic came to her because "there was a need and no one to help," she said.

The attractive girl, who has a nursing degree from Georgetown University, went into Biafra last month. At that time she had the option to leave the country by way of the rebel airstrip at Uli, but she elected to stay and work where she felt she was needed most.

Paul's heart skipped at least one beat when he read the article. Then he read it again, slowly. He had to believe it then, though he said, "My God, I saw her not two months ago. She didn't even hint at trying something like this."

"It was a shock to everyone, especially her parents," Dodson said.

"I'm sure," Paul said, looking at Dodson, still holding the article. "This doesn't exactly fit into the ambassador's diplomatic scenario, I shouldn't think."

"Nor her scenario for a long and happy life." Dodson retrieved the article from Paul's hand. "I understand you knew her."

"We were very close at one time." Paul wanted the subject dropped.

"When was the last time you saw her?"

"Two months ago. I was traveling through Lagos on my way here. I had been inspecting an earth station site in an area near Port Harcourt for a few months. Things started to get really bad down there and I decided it was time to leave. I just saw her for the one day in Lagos...." His voice trailed off. He didn't want to talk any more, but he had to ask. "How the hell did she get into Biafra?"

"I'm coming to that," Dodson said. He gulped the last of his coffee. "I guess she quickly tired of the expatriate swimming pool/club life in Lagos. You knew that she had been trained as a nurse in the States. Well, after a while, she started working at a Catholic hospital in Lagos and the next thing she was in Port Harcourt working at a mission hospital."

"I never heard a word about that." Paul was stuttering from his shock. "I can't imagine her father encouraging or even agreeing to her going down there."

"He didn't," Dodson said. "But she got so involved with her hospital work that she postponed going home to the States with her parents when they left Lagos. They planned to travel leisurely through Europe, and I understand that she promised to follow them home in a month or two, or as soon as the people at the mission advised her to leave.

"However, she never showed. Instead, she went into Biafra and got involved with the mission activities there."

"Helping the Ibos," Paul said. Then he muttered to himself, "Maybe she had a thing on the Ibos."

Dodson heard Paul's comment. "She did know an Ibo priest," he said. "As far as I know, she had been in contact with him at least three times while she was still in Lagos. His name is Father Okeke, kind of a charismatic figure who's been sneaking in and out of Biafra and traveling the world, raising money for the Ibos. He's doing a very good job of it, too."

The details about the priest upset Paul greatly. He bolted from his chair, startling Dodson, and stopped at the front door.

"What is it?" Dodson asked.

"I'm sorry. It's personal," Paul said, looking into the blackness of the new night. "It makes sense," he said then, facing Dodson. "She's just the type to try something like this."

Dodson thought he'd be prying if he asked Paul to explain what he meant, so he didn't ask. "We assume the priest was probably trying to get her to persuade her father to use his influence to somehow get the U.S. Government to help the Ibos. But there's more, Paul.

"There was a big federal drive about a month ago. A lot of villages were re-taken from the rebels and the whole rebel-controlled territory has shrunk substantially. Port Harcourt, which was Biafra's last link with the outside world, has fallen."

As he spoke, Dodson took a map from his briefcase and spread it over the coffee table. Paul walked slowly back across the room.

Dodson continued. "This is all that is left of Biafra now," he said, pointing to a small area circled with a heavy blue line. "The rebel airstrip at Uli is right in the center of this territory. There's an old rubber plantation near the airport which is now serving essentially as the headquarters for what is left of the Biafran government. This creek adjoins the plantation and runs all the way down into the delta."

Dodson stopped talking as he traced his finger over the thin blue line that represented the creek until it reached a maze of tiny dots representing the islands of the Rivers area.

Paul interrupted. "There's Adonni," he said, pointing to a dot closer to Port Harcourt. "That's near where I was working, but that's in federal territory."

"It is and it isn't," Dodson said. "That whole Rivers area is one of the places that has been difficult for the federals to hold onto. The only gains that the rebels have made in the past six months have been down in the delta. These northern troops don't fight well down there and they can't get their big guns and supplies in very easily. And on top of all that, the place is so filled with juju that federal soldiers, and even some officers, are leery of going in there."

"I know about the juju," Paul said. "There are cults down there that would make a juju man's eyes pop out."

Dodson would have liked to hear Paul's stories of the juju, but there wasn't time. He had to finish the briefing.

"Anyway," he said, redirecting their attention to the map, "our last report on Miss Cahill is that newspaper article. As far as we know, she is still working at Bugamu Island here," he said, indicating a spot on the map in the heart of the Rivers area. "It's about twelve hours by pirogue from Uli, as the article mentioned."

"Has that area fallen into rebel hands?"

"Pretty much," Dodson answered. "That's one of the reasons we're worried about her." He folded the map, leaving it on the table, and sat back in his chair. "In the last month and a half, the rebels have taken severe losses everywhere except in the Rivers area. Desertion and starvation are plaguing the rebel army. It's reported that numbers of deserters have formed armed bands that have been raiding hospitals, stealing food and even killing relief workers."

Paul was weak with sadness for the Ibos and for Maureen. "It doesn't sound too promising," he half whispered.

Dodson agreed. "But the rebels can't hold on much longer. The federal forces are now poised for a final drive into what's left of rebel territory. The Rivers area will be the focus of their final operation. First they'll soften it up with artillery and bombings, then they'll go in for the kill."

Dodson paused for a moment, then pointed at the map to emphasize his words. "You see, Paul, they have to get the airport at Uli, and in order to do that, they'll hit it from both sides, north and south, in a kind of pincers movement.

"Paul, what I'm telling you must be kept in the strictest confidence."

Paul didn't have to be told; he was offended that Dodson thought he should be warned.

"The point is, Paul," Dodson continued, "When the federal troops take over, which they will, it's merely a matter of time, they'll send in the Third Marine Commando Division, as they have in every other big operation. And those guys have a reputation for ruthlessness. They won't treat the relief workers kindly. They'll probably consider them to be rebels."

Paul didn't want to hear any more, but he knew he must listen for Maureen's sake. He began pacing the rug, eyeing the ancient Persian designs. Dodson's voice had begun to grate on him.

"The situation has deteriorated to the point where to remain there any longer would be to desire suicide. Of course, she wouldn't know what's coming. Even if she did, it would be impossible for her to get out alone."

Paul leaned against the front door, his back to Dodson, looking for anything visible in the night. "What can I do?" he asked, knowing there was very little help he could offer.

Dodson was obviously glad that Paul had asked. "We have a plan to get her out. You're involved in it. That's why I'm here.

"We need someone to go down there and bring her out. We would like you to do it." Dodson gave Paul time to digest what he had said.

"We know you're planning to go into Biafra soon and we want you to do what you can to help her get out while you're there. The airstrip is located near a creek which joins the tributary leading into the Rivers area. From the rebel airport at Uli to the mission hospital at Bugamu takes, as you've read, about twelve hours by pirogue. The whole operation shouldn't take more than a couple of days. Bring her back to the airport, and we'll fly you both to the island of Sao Tome or Fernando Poo. From there she can get back to the States and so can you, if you like. Or we can fly you back here to the plateau."

Paul remained silent, staring out the window. He developed a pessimistic attitude whenever he thought about going south. When he considered going into Biafra, he became absolutely fatalistic. At times he wished he had not made the commitment to inspect the earth station sites in the south, but then he remembered the financial compensation and the usual shortness of the visits. He tried not to think of it, but he knew that he would be going again soon.

Dodson interrupted Paul's thoughts, and Paul was grateful.

"Time is our biggest concern in this deal," the consul said. "No one knows how long the rebel airport will be able to operate. The federals will try to bring it down as soon as possible. After that, no one will be able to get into that area." He stopped talking long enough to take out a package of American cigarettes. He offered one to Paul, but Paul declined. Dodson lighted one for himself.

"You know, world public opinion is running against the federal government in this war," he said, blowing smoke toward the ceiling. "There have been reports of all kinds of atrocities against civilians living in rebel territory occupied by the federal army. And, of course, the starvation of millions of Ibo children is being blamed on the federal government. The rebels have been getting a pretty good press around the world, but as soon as that airport falls, the most favorable news accounts won't be worth a damn."

Paul had turned the porch light on. A swarm of large sausage flies began flying around the yellow bulb, crashing into the ceiling, losing their flimsy, cellophane like wings and falling to the cement floor. Soon the floor was covered with writhing flies.

"Surely there are people who are expert at what you're asking me to do." Paul said with some guilt, but without turning around.

"I suppose there are," Dodson replied. "But we don't have any working for us. We're down to a skeleton crew. And to be honest, Paul, we don't want this to be official. Besides, there are few Americans in the country better qualified than you to do this job. You know the area, you can get in and out fast, and you speak the language. If anyone can get her out alive, it's you. It only means one extra day for you down there."

Paul supposed all that was true. The idea both repulsed and intrigued him.

Dodson saw that Paul was weakening. "Besides, if you don't go, no one else will," he said, unleashing his last psychological weapon. "It won't be long before the only people who are going to survive Biafra are those on the last boat out. And that boat's going to be leaving very soon. Will you go?"

Paul knew he had been persuaded; he had known it from the moment Dodson mentioned her name.

"Hell, I might as well," he sighed, trying to appear nonchalant. "I'll be there anyway."

The steward came into the room just then and announced, "Chop is ready, sir."

"Good, Ali. *Abinci dai kyau?* "Paul asked, escorting Dodson to the dining room. "*Sannu da Aiki.*"

"*To, mun gode da Allah, abinci dai kyau,*" Ali replied. Huge grins spread over both their faces.

"*Na gode,*" Paul said.

They seated themselves at the table.

"Oh, there's one thing more," Dodson said, sliding his chair closer to the table.

Paul had almost lost his appetite. In the past he had tried to avoid thinking of her; now it was forced upon him.

"What else?"

"There's a young American Protestant missionary who has also disappeared into Biafra. His father has written his congressman and we've been asked, the consulate in Kaduna, to see what we can do. I'm wondering if while you're down there you can check on him as well."

"Are they together?"

"Not to my knowledge. I've just heard that he's gone down there and we'd like to get him out too, for the same reasons."

"Do you have any idea where he is?"

"I'm afraid I can't be too helpful on that score, but when you get to Uli you can ask around. I'll give you the particulars before you leave. Do what you can, but remember the girl is our first concern."

"I'll remember."

CHAPTER VII

Uli, Biafra, December 22, 1969.

It was just getting light when Paul awoke. He dressed and crossed the overgrown lawn behind the compound which sloped into a creek fifty yards in back of the house. He stood rigid on the small wooden platform that jutted into the placid, brown water. The air was heavy, filled with the damp, cool sweetness of the early African morning. His eyes followed the creek to the bank of mangrove some fifteen yards away. The creek disappeared into it. A fine mist was rising from the water.

He's late, Paul though, glancing at his watch. After living in Nigeria for two years, he still could not get used to the inability of people to stay on schedule. Paul wondered if his man would come. It had cost him fifty pounds in bribes to get a boat. Until then, the minister's preparations for the flight south and the relief flight to Uli had worked out precisely as planned. Paul had finished his inspection of the earth terminal site in one day, and he was eager to devote his full energies to the only mission that mattered to him.

The sound of an engine in the distance broke the dawn silence. Paul looked in the direction of the sound and saw the pirogue emerge from the jungle like a long, black log. As the boat neared the platform, the boatman cut the engine and Paul grabbed the prow to keep it from knocking against the pilings.

Paul greeted the man who was squatting near the ancient outboard motor. *"Gina bu akagi."*

"Aha m bu, Moonshine." The boatman spoke his name loudly and strongly. He was separated from Paul by a small passenger compartment which was simply nine by seven square feet of thin tin roofing supported by six two-by fours nailed to the sides of the boat.

"Yes!" Moonshine announced proudly in his high-pitched voice. "I speak English proper."

Paul lashed the pirogue to the dock and Moonshine climbed along the side of the boat, causing it to tilt sharply to one side in the water. He jumped nimbly onto the landing. He was not very tall, a little over five feet, and he was wearing a pair of oil-stained tennis shoes, frayed shorts, and a dark blue sweatshirt with UNIVERSITY OF OK-LAHOMA printed in faded letters on its front.

"I am Moonshine," the ebony-colored man said again, and he grinned widely, revealing beautifully white teeth. "I am coming for you."

"How much to take me to Bugamu?" Paul asked.

"Plenty palavar there, plenty palavar," Moonshine shrieked.

"Skip the palavar; how much?"

"Fifty pounds."

"Too much."

Moonshine turned to undo the lashings'

"Final price," Paul said flatly, "fifteen pounds."

Moonshine continued undoing the lashings. With that, Paul picked up his bag and started back toward the end of the dock toward the house.

"Okay, okay," Moonshine shouted after him. "Twenty pounds. I take you for twenty pounds. How you like that?"

Paul climbed into the boat without another word about the price and sat opposite Moonshine on one of the small benches on each side of the tin roof.

Moonshine used a long pole to push the pirogue away from the dock, and the boat slid silently into the brackish water. The boatman whipped the silver-painted engine that hung over the stern like some great relic. After three tries it started and the boat headed downstream. Paul watched the house disappear as they rounded the first bend of mangrove.

At first the creek was narrow and milky brown, with many tributaries, but as they traveled south it widened into the Niger River. The lush mangrove was replaced by banks were topped by tree-covered hills that obliterated the view of the horizon. The sun was still low in the morning sky, but already the back of Paul's shirt was wet with sweat. Where the river was wide the boat glided downstream even though the engine performed erratically, sometimes speeding up so that it shook in its mountings, then slowing to a disturbed wheeze and sounding as if it were about to die.

The thought of seeing her again brought back the old longing, something he had tried to repress and at which he had been only moderately successful. He wondered how she would react to his being there. They had not seen each other since that night at her father's party, the night he walked out on her. He tried to gauge his own feelings and he wondered what his reaction would be when he saw her again. Unwillingly the old emotions she caused in him rose from within his depths.

By noon they were nearing the delta region and the river had narrowed again into a maze of creeks that fed an endless forest of mangrove. The whole area had become a swamp formed by the Niger River on its way to the sea. They passed through places where the bright green sudd grew so thick that the water was almost invisible. A carpet of roots stretched from bank to bank. Traveling became agonizingly slow, and there was no wind to relieve the intense, stale heat that enveloped them. Twice during their journey the pirogue was brought to a standstill. At times the forest formed a canopy which sprinkled bright, yellow-green slivers of light into the water.

The heat became oppressive in the early afternoon. Sitting under the tin roof, Paul felt that he was inside an oven. He had moved into the sun earlier but that was far worse. At least the roof afforded protection from the scorching rays. By late afternoon it began to cool slightly, but mosquitoes came with the cooler air. Paul cursed himself for not bringing repellent, but after a while he stopped caring and only slapped at those insects he could see feasting on his legs and arms.

"I smell the sea," Paul said with immense gratitude as they passed a wide junction in the river. Nothing had ever smelled better to him, and for a moment he could feel on his face the gentle caress of fresh, salt air.

"Follow that river to ocean," Moonshine said, pointing at a tributary that led into the mangrove.

Paul nodded. "We must be very near the ocean now. I had no idea it was this close."

After about an hour, the island village of Bugamu appeared around a bend ahead in the river. The village was a little larger than the others they had seen on their way. Small clusters of mud and straw huts stood on stilts on the muddy river bank. Beyond, tin-roofed structures lined a road that led from the dock through the village and into the jungle. The entire village glowed with an unearthly, rose-colored light created by the setting sun.

As their pirogue pulled into shore, Paul jumped onto the dock and Moonshine threw his bag up to him. "Tomorrow morning at seven," Paul said, pointing at his watch, which the boatman had been admiring.

Moonshine nodded vigorously and jumped out of the boat to tie it to the landing. "I be here, I sleep here," he said.

"Good. Until tomorrow."

Paul started for the village. A small, almost naked boy with the distended belly that Paul had noticed on most of the children in the area stood on the edge of the dock. He seemed to be the only person in the village. The dirt road leading from the dock to the market was deserted. But Paul thought he heard drums in the distance, rhythmic and exciting, coming from the jungle. The boy approached Paul and touched his hand.

Paul squatted down to the small boy's level. The child couldn't have been more than seven years old. He was a light cocoa color and his hair had tinges of red which Paul knew was one of the signs of kwashiorkor.

"What is your name?" Paul asked, not really expecting an answer.

"Hyacinth," came the reply softly.

"Hyacinth," Paul repeated surprised.

The boy smiled. Paul put his hand on the boy's shoulder.

You know *bakimbo* madam, madam doctor?" Paul asked.

"*Mata bakimbo*," the boy said, nodding slowly and smiling. He stared at Paul with hollow eyes. "*Mata bakimbo*," he said again. His voice was weak but audible.

Paul followed the boy up the main dirt road that led between the empty market stalls. The stench from the marketplace struck him mercilessly as they passed and he was glad when they were beyond it. The boy led him into an alleyway that wound behind the market to a wide path that narrowed as it cut among the tiny huts that smelled of smoke and rotting fish. Paul heard people moving and talking behind the curtained doorways of their homes, but it was not a typical village where people crowded unabashedly around a stranger.

Finally the boy and Paul came to a large, two-story house which, in the fading light, appeared to be painted yellow. It seemed curiously out of place on the island. Made of cinder blocks, with a flat roof, it was the largest structure in the village, built at the edge of the jungle and facing the river. It was surrounded by a dilapidated six-foot fence made of rusty, corrugated iron sheets used for roofing. The gate was rusted permanently open.

The boy led Paul to the gate and pointed to the cement stairway at the side of the house that led up to the second story.

"Madam, *bakimbo*," Hyacinth said.

Paul gave the boy a pound. He looked at the red note in euphoric disbelief, then bowed grandly to Paul and started back to the village.

Paul hesitated, looking after the child, before going through the gate. The yard, overgrown with jungle ferns, sloped down to the river where it ended at a wall of corrugated iron. Gigantic wild hibiscus, losing their red color in the pink glow of evening, and white frangipanis flourished against the length of the wall.

Paul took a deep breath and finally climbed the stairs. The door at the top was open. He knocked and entered the kitchen which was faintly lit by a kerosene lantern and smelled of wet cement.

"Maureen?"

A male voice answered, "Yes, sir."

Paul looked to where he thought the voice was coming from. Through the dimness he could see a black

69

boy squatting before a large pot of water, preparing yams.

The boy stood up when he saw Paul. "Madam not here," he said.

Paul's heart jumped in his chest. He felt suddenly afraid for Maureen.

"Where is madam?"

"Madam at hospital, working," the houseboy said as he approached Paul. "I am Sunday, madam's steward. Madam be home soon." The boy reached for Paul's bag. "You welcome here, sir."

"Thank you, Sunday. I'm Mr. Jeffries," Paul said. For the first time he was glad that he had come and he relaxed.

He followed Sunday, who carried his bag and the kerosene lantern, into the living room. Large and comfortable, the room was separated from the kitchen by a bookcase. Brightly colored throw rugs and bamboo mats covered the floor. A French window opened onto a tiny balcony facing the river. A desk was placed against the wall with a side to the window so that, while working, one could be inspired by the stunning landscape. Paintings hung on the other walls. The only light in the room came from the small lantern and the red glow of sunset which had turned the clouds a brilliant crimson.

Paul went to the window. The river mirrored the flaming sky, looking like a molten lava flow as it cut its path through the black mangrove.

"Sir, do you wish to take a bath?"

Sunday's question startled Paul. "Bath?" he said, turning to the boy. "You have a bathtub here?"

"Yes, sir, very fine bathtub! I fix water for you," Sunday said. He disappeared into a room near the kitchen.

The ancient bathtub, like some relic from a Roman temple, seemed as out of place here as the house itself. The water was cool and slightly rust-colored, and it had the musty odor that all water in this part of the country seemed to have, but it felt sublime to Paul. After bathing, he donned the change of clothes he had brought and returned to the living room. He sat on the sofa facing the window. It was now very dark outside, but the room glowed from a brightly burning tilly lamp that Sunday had placed on top of the bookcase.

Paul heard Maureen before he saw her. Sunday spoke to someone in the kitchen, and Paul knew, without distinguishing her voice, that it was she. He stood up when she came into the room, feeling slightly nervous.

She was as he had remembered her, but something was different. She was wearing her thick, dark blond hair in pageboy fashion, parted on one side. And her large blue-green eyes, which had always fascinated him, were strange: softer, yet brighter, with a hint of the haggard look that he had seen before in the eyes of expatriates who had spent too much time in country. She was wearing a one-piece dress made of a silken material, so light that he could trace the outline of her breasts. In the dampness of the heat, the dress clung to her. Its hem ended two inches above her knees, revealing her long, shapely legs. Paul could see that she was wearing a half-slip underneath the dress. She had lost some weight since he had last seen her, but she still moved gracefully, with that athletic quality that had made her such a talented tennis player. He had forgotten just how beautiful she was.

Her full, delicately formed lips parted into an honest smile when she saw him.

Paul spoke softly. "Surprised?"

"I was expecting . . . . "

"Someone else?"

71

"Certainly not you, Paul! I thought you were on the plateau, or even in the States by now."

"I'm still living on the plateau. Think I'll stay there forever," he said.

"This is really a surprise. I don't get many guests." She welcomed him with a friendly hug. He had forgotten what her touch did to him.

"Maybe it's your neighborhood. It's rather out of the way." Paul quipped, trying to mask the effect she had on him. Her calm and femininity seemed as natural as ever to him, even in that Godforsaken place.

Maureen smiled again. She couldn't believe that he was sitting in her living room.

She moved to the sofa. "How did you get here?" she asked.

"I came up on the African Queen," Paul said, leaning back in the chair that faced her across the coffee table.

She laughed and, after a pause, said, "I guess the more appropriate question is, why?"

Paul became serious. "I could ask you the same question," he said.

Maureen was quick to answer. "An Ibo priest brought me here a month ago."

"Why here, for God's sake?"

"I guess because it has all the amenities. It's also out of the way," she said. She stood up, put her hands on her hips, and arched her back in a half stretch. "Besides," she groaned, "it's got a tre-e-e-mendous view." She stayed at the window, staring at the night.

Paul knew that she hadn't told him the real reason. "I'm afraid the view may be marred soon," he said dryly.

She didn't respond and kept her back to him.

"Can't you see what's going to happen? Have you no idea of what's going on in this country?"

72

She turned quickly to face him and for a moment her eyes flashed. "I know there's a war, if that's what you mean," she said angrily.

"But what you don't know is that this whole area," he said, making a sweeping gesture with his arm toward the window and beyond, "is going to be the center of the biggest federal drive of the war. And the fact that you are working with rebels makes *you* a rebel, as far as the federal government is concerned."

She did not seem concerned, turning and looking out the window again. "Paul, I've been here for one month and nothing has happened. This place is so isolated. No one ever comes here." She spoke with her back to him.

"Not isolated enough." He talked loudly and quickly, to be sure that she heard him. "You'll be right in the heart of it. Things have been quiet in the last three months because the federal army has been massing in Port Harcourt in preparation for the big advance."

"You know an awful lot about the government," she said, a bit sarcastically, intentionally changing the subject. "You're still working for them?"

"I'm an independent contractor. I have a contract with the federal government of Nigeria. You know that, Maureen!"

There was a long pause.

"For Christ's sake!" Paul erupted, finally breaking the cool silence. "What do you want me to do, quit my work and take up the Ibo cause? Who do you think is going to be running this country a month from now? It sure ain't going to be the Ibos!"

He moved out of the pool of light cast by the lamp to where she stood in silhouette against the window.

"And like it or not, Maureen, these people are entering the age of technology. They need a modern telecommunications system. My God, girl, you've got to live within the realm of the possible."

"You sound like my father," Maureen said with some contempt. The soft light from the lantern on the other side of the room erased the tired look from her face, and she appeared more beautiful than Paul had ever seen her.

"Your father is a realist," he said quietly.

"I know, but I suppose I thought at one time that . . . ." She tried to conceal it, but her voice revealed frustration and despair.

"What?" Paul tried not to sound too impatient.

"I was thinking of the realists, the businessmen who used to come to the embassy in Lagos. They were all the same. The news of oil discoveries and reports that the war couldn't last much longer drew them like magnets to this poor country. And they remained oblivious to the fact that people were starving not two hundred miles away. It wasn't that they didn't care; they weren't even aware!

"And U.S. policy reflected this attitude: 'Don't rock the boat; don't recognize Biafra; ignore the war.' After a while I couldn't stand the heartlessness of my countrymen, and I couldn't be a part of what they were allowing to happen."

"What alternative do you propose, Maureen? Send in the marines?"

"I don't know, but more could have been done diplomatically." She paused to get control of herself. "What's the use?"

"What do you mean?"

"It's too late!" she sighed. "The only hope now is for some kind of negotiated settlement."

Paul picked up the picture of Maureen and her parents that was on the desk and held it as if it were precious. Happier days, he said to himself.

"You know, Maureen, you've changed," he remarked after a moment. "You are very different from the girl I knew in Lagos and on the plateau."

"We've both changed, Paul," she said. She was plainly tired. "You walked out of my life three months ago without so much as a 'See you around'."

He looked at her and their eyes met. A bitter smile played on his lips. He wanted to say something but he thought he shouldn't.

"Why did you come back, Paul?"

"I came because I was sent here on business. The minister of communications in Kaduna asked me to come to Uli to look at a site for a proposed earth station. I wasn't even aware that you were here until the counsul in Kaduna told me. I thought you'd be home by now."

She walked through the arc of lamplight to the couch, and he noticed a weariness about her that he had never seen before. It frightened him. She seemed older.

"Just stopping by on your way somewhere else?" she asked, sitting and putting her feet up.

"On my way home," he answered.

"Back to the bastion of colonialism, the plateau. What do they call it?" she asked with a forced smile that showed again a desire to change the subject.

"Hill Station."

She watched the flickering kerosene flame.

"I was afraid you didn't like the plateau," he said sarcastically. "It's pretty tame and probably a deadly bore compared to this place and it's so colonial. And there's precious little opportunity there for one to become a martyr."

He wanted to go to her, take her in his arms and make love to her, but he couldn't forget what she had done to him. "You look tired," he said instead.

"Yes, I am. I must go to bed. Have to get up very early." She stood up, and he knew their conversation was over.

"You have no idea . . .," he began anyway.

"I simply can't leave now, Paul. I appreciate your coming here. I know it took a great deal of courage. But you don't know what we're doing here. You can't be expected to, because you're not involved. You haven't seen the hospital. If I left now, the children would have no one. All of them have lost their parents. I'm all they've got now. I had to leave some children behind at the mission in Port Harcourt and I will never do that again."

"That may all be true," he said, "but I don't see why you have to be so involved." His eyes caught hers again. "I'm really beginning to think you've got a martry complex."

"That's not true," she snapped back. "I'll tell you, very simply, why I'm involved: because if I weren't nobody would be!" A tense pause followed.

"Well, I tried," Paul said after a few moments. "I'll tell you one thing, Maureen, I'm leaving this island tomorrow for the plateau. It was probably a mistake for me to come."

She looked as though she had just been slapped. "I'll show you to your room," she said coldly, picking up the lantern from the bookcase.

Paul followed her into a small bedroom which was overwhelmed by a large double bed surrounded by white mosquito neeting.

"I'll leave the light here," she said. "I can find the way to my room in the dark. Turn off the light when you like. Good night."

"Good night, Maureen," he said, and she left the room quickly, closing the door behind her. He felt frustrated and awkward and angry.

Taking off his clothes and pulling loose the mosquito netting, which was tucked under the mattress, Paul realized he was exhausted from his long journey. He smothered the light and eased his body between the clean sheets which had the same heavy, musty odor as the room. He drew the net around him. In the black silence he could hear the drone of the mosquitoes as they divebombed against the net.

He was upset by the new air about Maureen, the disquieting remoteness that belongs to someone who has had a profound personal and spiritual experience and is irrevocably different. He wondered if Maureen had had such an experience, and if he would ever be able to know her again. The last thing he wondered before falling asleep was whether a mosquito was inside the net with him.

CHAPTER VIII

Bugamu, Biafra, December 23, 1969.

The barking of a village dog woke Paul just as the first strands of morning light were penetrating the curtained window of his room. It was not the fireball sunrise of the plateau but rather a soft, gradual brightening of the greyness. The river appeared shrouded in a white mist and the tree tops protruded above the cloud cover.

Paul felt he should leave early, without a word to Maureen. He had not been prepared for her reaction to his visit. He had expected a warm welcome and some expression of a desire to get back together. But he thought she exhibited only a very mild interest in their relationship. He knew her well enough to realize that it would be futile to continue to try to persuade her to change her mind about leaving.

He dressed quietly and hurriedly and, with the strengthening dawn, left the house. When he reached the boat, the mist was already rising from the water. Moonshine was curled, like a large, black dog, on a bench under the tin roof.

Paul called to him. The boatman stirred, stretched his arms and legs while still lying on his side, then sat up, rubbing his eyes.

"We go now, Moonshine," Paul announced.

Moonshine nooded. Without a word he moved in a half-crouch toward the bow. He jumped onto the dock, pulled the boat close for Paul to climb aboard, and hopped back in after untying the lashing and shoving the boat away from the dock with his powerful legs. Paul focused on the sad village, which slowly fell away from view, as Moonshine poled the boat toward the deeper water.

An hour later, when the mist had been burned off by the glaring sun and they had reached the widest junctun in the river, a boat approached them from the opposite direction. The vessels passed no closer than fifty feet, but Paul recognized Larry sitting near the bow. Both the missionary and his boatman waved, and Paul and Moonshine waved back. Paul knew that Larry was on his way to Bugamu, though Maureen had not mentioned him. Paul wondered what their relationship was. As he watched Larry's boat disappear around a bend in the river. He decided to have Moonshine return them to Bugamu. But almost as quickly he realized the futility of such a move. Perhaps Larry could convince her to leave, he thought with some bitterness.

By four o'clock that afternoon Paul was back on the plantation. He got a hop from Uli to Fernando Po and soon after six that evening he was at the luxurious New Government Hotel in Port Harcourt, enjoying the security of civilization. In his hotel room he drafted the telegram he would send to the minister the next morning, informing him that the earth station site at Uli was perfect and that negotiations for the sixth station should be concluded promptly. He had finished making plans for being on the first flight to the plateau by the time he went to bed, weary and depressed from the personal events of the last few days.

He awoke with a start. It took him a moment to realize where he was. The late morning sun was streaming through the curtains that hung over the window of his air-conditioned room. He thought immediately of Maureen, of his fruitless visit.

He hoped he was going to be able to put her out of his mind at last after he had seen her in Biafra, but seeing her had only reinforced his feelings for her. He pictured Larry travling upriver and he wondered if they had spent the night together. He wondered if Larry would try to persuade her to leave or if Larry himself was aware of the danger.

Paul had no choice but to walk the mile back to the hotel from the Post and Telegraph in the heart of the business section across town where he had gone to send his message to the minister. He couldn't help but notice the changes that had taken place since he was last there. The city had been transformed into an armed camp. The streets were deserted, most of the shops were closed, and the windows of some of the larger stores were partially boarded over. He passed a few self-styled militiamen wearing multicolored homemade uniforms carrying guns and intimidating people at every opportunity.

He was on the deserted main road when he heard singing in the distance. It reminded him of a church hymn, and he thought it must be coming from a school somewhere, although he knew that all the schools had been closed for months.

The singing grew louder. Suddenly, ahead, Paul could see two loose columns of soldiers approaching the bridge spanning a small river that flowed through the downtown section. He did not want to meet the soldiers on that narrow bridge, but he had no choice. To stop abruptly or to turn around would look suspicious.

He reached one end of the bridge just as the soldiers reached the other. He knew it was probably the dreaded Third Marine Commandos. The bridge had no sidewalk, just a kind of large curb against the low wall. He could see that the troops, who crowded the street, were not going to move for him, so he got up on the curb and continued walking as nonchalantly as possible. As the soldiers approached, their singing no longer reminded him of a hymn but rather of a lusty marching song. Each soldier was carrying an automatic weapon and, although they didn't stop, they turned to stare at him as they passed.

The last soldier turned completely around while marching and leered at Paul over his automatic weapon. Paul felt strange and cold, as though he were very close to death. He knew that his slightest move could be interpreted as provocation. He also knew that other expatriates had been caught in the middle and killed, and he had heard stories of killings and rapings in the outlying expatriate missions.

He watched the troops disappear into the distance. As they marched away, their singing again assumed the haunting quality of a hymn.

CHAPTER IX

Bugamu, Biafra, December 27, 1969.

"We go for island," Moonshine said. He stood on the dock looking down at Paul in the pirogue that rocked and shifted as he moved about, making final preparations for the trip. It was the first time in his life that Paul had acted purely on impulse. He had no reason to believe that Maureen would change her mind. He knew that she would most likely resent his efforts, yet he also knew that he had to try harder to get her out.

"Plenty palavar," Moonshine said, shaking his head. His ebony face was dotted with little beads of sweat. Paul waved a wad of red and blue bills for Moonshine to see.

"You work for me now, Moonshine. I pay you proper," he said.

The boatman eyed the money shrewdly. "How much you pay me?"

"You work for me for one week more, and I will give you fifty pounds," Paul said.

Moonshine's eyes widened slowly and he smiled. Paul didn't want to bargain with him. The money meant nothing to him now.

"Let's get going," he ordered, stuffing the money back into the pocket of his shorts.

The sky was covered with low clouds and the air was damp and heavy. The grey-yellow morning light washed out the natural colors of the landscape and gave the scene an eerie quality. They hadn't gone far when the rain began.

Paul crawled under the tin roof. Moonshine rigged an old umbrella over the spot where he sat and slowed the engine to idle. The boat moved slowly ahead. The raindrops, large and warm and heavy, increased in intensity until they beat down on the roof with such force that they drowned out the rumble of the distant thunder. The rain exploded into the yellow water, blurring the surface, and river and sky seemed to blend as one.

By late afternoon they had passed Andonni village. The rain, which had stopped earlier, had slowed them down, and Paul doubted they would get to Bugamu before nightfall. The village appeared quiet, too quiet; there were no boats at the dock and no children playing along the banks. The only sound was the erratic put-put of the outboard engine.

It was dark when they arrived at Bugamu. When they landed Paul saw that Moonshine was frightened. He knew that the fear of the juju was greater in him than fear of the enemy. A vague apprehension took hold of Paul as the pirogue knocked against the pilings. He jumped onto the dock and, as he secured the bowline, heard stirrings from another large pirogue that was already tied up. He looked hard through the dark but could see nothing, yet he was aware of the presence of the boatman in the other pirogue. Moonshine shouted to the stranger in a river dialect that Paul did not understand.

"That man say he work for other *bakimbo*," Moonshine said. "Other *bakimo* go with madam *bakimbo* to her house. This man will sleep in the boat."

The announcement that Maureen and Larry were together did not come as a shock to Paul. He gave the lashings a final tug to make sure that they were secure, then stretched his body. The night was breathless, black velvet that smothered the stars in its folds. The air was damp and cool and smelled musty. It came as a welcome relief from the scorching heat of the day.

"Paul, Paul Jeffries!" A man's voice, loud and familiar, came from the dark. Then the man stepped into the light of a torch Paul was holding.

"Am I glad to see you!" Larry exclaimed, shaking Paul's hand with a grip that confirmed his words. "Maureen told me that you were here but had left yesterday."

"I almost had, but I decided to come back."

"I saw you on the river the other morning."

"And prior to that, the last time I saw *you* was at the club," Paul reminded him. "What happened? How'd you ever end up here?"

"Oh, I was up there for a while, but things didn't work out."

"What happened?"

"You mean about the clinic? The land at Barakin Ladi?"

"Yes. After I saw you, I mentioned it to my friend, the Minister of Communications. He said he would check on it."

"Thanks, Paul. So much has happened since then. This is where I'm needed now."

"I was just getting ready to sack out," Paul said, motioning toward the boat.

"Not there, I hope I'm on my way to our little clinic on the other side of the island. Why don't you come along? There's an extra bed. Besides, you haven't seen the place yet."

The thought of sleeping on a bed rather than on the hard boat bench was too tempting to resist. "I'd like to see the clinic," Paul said.

"Good, let's go."

The two men walked over the old wooden dock to the shore, guided by the small spot of light provided by the torch.

"I'm very excited about the possibilities here," Larry said as they passed the village huts along the narrow passageways. "I think I told you at the club that my father is retiring in June, my brother is completing his last year in the seminary, and my sister is graduating from college. My father wants to settle here and become involved in our church's missionary activities. He plans to use his retirement money to help out."

They walked through the dark, deserted market stalls, and then the road cut through the jungle. With each step Paul expected to land on a soft, large, round body of the poisonous adders that came out to feed at night.

"Why would you let your family come here?" Paul asked. "It's not safe for anyone."

"Paul, for the past four weeks I've been making the rounds of the villages of Andonni, Abonnema and Bugamu. I spend a day at each village. In the morning I attend to what medical needs the people have and in the afternoon I'm able to give an hour or so of Bible studies." He spoke with excitement and conviction.

"I'm gaining the people's confidence. The really sick children are being cared for at the clinic. It's the only thing that even remotely resembles a hospital, and I can spend a few days a week here, looking after them."

"But doesn't that put an added burden on Maureen?"

"She's doing a marvelous job. I hope that she'll stay on after my family comes."

"You like her very much, don't you?"

Larry didn't answer. Ahead, Paul could make out a dimly lighted structure which he presumed was the clinic. He wondered if Maureen would be there.

"Larry," he said, "I don't know if you know, but this whole area is soon going to be in the middle of the biggest battle of the war. You wouldn't want to bring your family into that, would you?"

"Of course not, Paul! I know you mean well, but I don't agree. This area is too isolated. These river people are the only ones who know their way here. Besides, there's nothing strategically important here."

"That's not the point, Larry. It's a question of location. This area is an access way to Uli. That's where they want to get to. They'll come by air first, bombing and strafing, then the troops will march in. They *will* come. Don't doubt it. It's not just a bunch of juju cults."

"I really can't believe it will come this far, Paul. Anyway, it's still another six months until June. We'll know more by then."

'That may be too late."

By now they had reached the small building. Sunday greeted them at the door and when Larry handed him the flashlight, he set off for the village. Paul followed Larry into a room where a lantern was burning on a table. Paul was feeling the same frustration he had felt from talking to Marueen about leaving. He knew that his words were wasted on Larry.

The room had obviously once served as a classroom, for there was an old blackboard at one end. Children were all over the floor. A few of them sat propped against the wall, but most were lying on their sides on little straw mats. All of them stared vacantly at the walls and ceiling. Paul avoided their eyes, their pathetic stares, but he was glad to see them; their being alive gave him a strange feelling of reassurance. A small child in one corner was fussing, looking as though he wanted to cry out in pain but unable to do so because of the effort required. Paul watched Larry gently pick up the child and rock him in his arms.

"Do you remember what you called them?"

"Who?"

"The leper children on the plateau who begged in the Kingsway market."

Paul looked puzzled.

"Allah's pickin'. These are Allah's pickin'," Larry said almost exuberantly as he held the child and motioned around the room. His touch seemed to have an almost immediate soothing effect upon the little boy. After a short time, Larry lay the child down, sound asleep.

Paul noticed that Larry's eyes quickly and expertly regarded all the children, then he picked up the lamp and directed Paul to follow him into an adjoining room.

"It's not much," he said, pointing to the two sagging beds in the room, "but it's a place to sleep." He put the lantern on a table near the door and dived onto his bed.

"It's far superior to that bench in the boat," Paul said, sitting on the other bed that was pushed against one wall and was partially covered with a mosquito net. He was happy to know that Larry and Maureen were not sleeping together.

Larry seemed lost in thought. His left leg was dangling over the edge of his bed and he was staring at the door.

"What's the matter, Larry?" Paul asked.

"Something you said," he answered.

"About the coming battle?"

"No, the juju. Paul, I've seen it and it frightens me."

"I didn't think you were superstitious."

"I'm not. But I don't know how to cope with it. It's the only thing I fear here, and the one thing that I'm working hardest to conquer. I don't want my family to see it. Some of the practices are so awful, so shocking."

"You can't change it, Larry."

"Don't say that," he replied angrily. He undid the mosquito net that was rolled above the mattress and walked to the table.

"Okay if I turn out the light now?"

"Fine," Paul said, removing his sandals and lying back on the bed. The light was put out and Paul heard Larry getting into his bed.

"The tragedy of the juju is that they take some elements of Christianity and twist them into something awful," Larry said in the darkness. For the first time Paul was aware of the genuine tone of horror in his voice.

CHAPTER X

Bugamu, Biafra, December 27, 1969.

Rain was pouring down, and warm, moist air wafted in through the open windows to Paul's bed. He opened his eyes. Through the gauzy haze of the mosquito netting, the morning light appeared yellow-ochre, washed with green. He looked over to Larry's bed. It was empty. The rain performed a muted crescendo on the iron roof.

"Larry, Larry!"

Her whisper and gentle knock was barely audible above the storm noises. The door was opened shyly, and Maureen entered.

"Paul!"

"Surprise!" he said, looking past her.

"What are you doing here? I thought you had left for good," she said, rolling up the netting of Larry's bed.

"That's what I keep asking myself," he said, without a trace of humor in his voice.

Paul propped himself up on his right elbow and the bed sheet fell to his waist, revealing his tanned, muscled torso.

He was thin but he had good shoulders, like a swimmer. He reached under the net to pick up his shorts from the floor near his bed, thinking that would be enough to make her leave so he could dress.

"Why did you come back?" she asked.

"I saw and heard a lot in Port Harcourt that made me realize how close the end is. The town is an armed camp. You don't see any civilians, just soldiers. They're ready for the final drive, Maureen."

Her hair was soaked, and the silk blouse that she wore tucked into her tan shorts clung to her fair skin, revealing the outline of her breasts. Her moist legs glistened, and Paul noticed little splotches of mud on her feet. She took a white towel that was hanging over the foot of Larry's bed and sat on the bed across from Paul to dry herself. He could smell the rain on her.

"Did you ever hear of a gentleman by the name of Colonel Barka?" He had forgotten he wanted to dress.

"No. Should I have?"

"He's from one of the Rivers tribes."

"What about him?"

"While I was in Port Harcourt I heard that the government had recruited a battalion from the Rivers tribes. Colonel Barka is their leader." Paul spoke as if repeating a piece of gossip he didn't really believe. "You don't seem very interested."

"I am."

"The federal forces want the River tribes on their side for two reasons," he said with the tone of a teacher being patient with an unmotivated pupil. "Because they know these creeks and swamps and because they are the traditional enemies of the Ibos. But so far they have remained neutral."

She patted her hair with the towel, then shook her head like a spirited horse shaking its mane.

"Just before Port Harcourt fell to federal forces, Colonel Barka led his men on a little raid on a hospital that was caring for Ibo soldiers. They not only slaughtered all the patients, they killed hospital personnel as well. I thought you might want to know."

"I think this must be the most horrible war ever," Maureen said quietly. Paul could see that the news had shocked her.

She stopped drying her hair and dropped the towel in her lap. It covered her shorts and accentuated the tan of her legs. She put her elbows on her thighs and, leaning forward, put her hands on the sides of her neck. She seemed weary, like the last time he had seen her.

"There's mud on your feet," he said after a while.

She looked down, crossed her legs, and leaned over to wipe the mud off her ankles and feet.

"You should know that Colonel Barka and his men are out on the rivers now," Paul said. "So if any strange people arrive on the island, and you are fortunate enough to see them coming, you'd better take to the bush!"

"But some of these children are children of the Rivers people!" she said excitedly. She was paying strict attention to him now.

"When the shooting starts, no one is going to ask questions." Paul spoke calmly, coldly. "Some of these children are Ibos, so you will be seen as aiding the Ibos. When this war is over, the Rivers people want to reap some of the financial and other benefits from the government. One of the ways to be sure to be rewarded is to help in the final drive. It's a sure-fire way of expressing loyalty without risking anything."

"Paul, I don't want to talk about it."

"Not talking about it is not going to solve anything!" Paul snapped the sheet back up to his chest and put his hands behind his neck against the pillow. "Where's Larry?" he asked.

91

"He must be on his rounds of the other villages."

Paul pictured Larry in his small boat out on the river in the rain. "Nothing stops him," he said, half to himself. "He's more reliable than the mailman."

She laughed feebly and began toweling her legs again.

"You love Larry?" Paul's words were so unexpected they surprised even him. He turned his head slightly, and their eyes met.

"Silence is assent," he said sadly. "He loves you, you know."

"No, I *don't* know," she said defiantly. "But how could anyone not love Larry?"

Here words puzzled him. They were spoken with feeling, but like an elliptical remark that is ambiguous.

"You're trying to make yourself like him," he said, not looking at her. "But deep down you're like me, though you'll never admit it. You want the finer things of life, but for some reason you resist as if they were evil."

"You're wrong," she cried out, shaking her head.

"I know you, Maureen, and I know that every minute you remain on this island you multiply the danger to yourself. You know that too, yet you stay on. You're putting up a brave front, but you're afraid. You were afraid that first night I saw you on the road. I saw the fear in your eyes — and you're still afraid."

He paused to allow her to reply. She said nothing.

"You're trying to convince yourself that you belong here, but you don't! Maybe Larry belongs here, but you don't. The only times you've been comfortable in this country were when you were surrounded by the luxury and security of the embassy in Lagos and at Hill Station, on the plateau with me. Now you've come to this goddamned place and taken up a lost cause, and for what?"

He studied her closely, trying to gauge from her expression if his words had any effect. He couldn't tell but he was convinced that he had judged her correctly. She still had that cool reserve, but he wasn't persuaded by it. He had seen her when her defenses were down.

At the same time, Paul knew that Larry had an extraordinary influence over her and he resented it. She seemed more natural, more at ease, since Larry had been there. He had never seen them together but he envied Larry's obviously intimate relationship with her. Larry would have been the last person Paul would have chosen for her. They were so different: she, beautiful, sophisticated, cool and detached; he, tall, angular, not very handsome, unsophisticated and totally committed to his beliefs. If there had not been a war, Paul was certain they would never have been brought together. He was convinced that if Larry weren't there he would be able to convince her to leave.

"Why don't you admit that you love Larry? That's why you're staying on!" Paul's jealousy was obvious now.

"I do love Larry, but in a way that you wouldn't understand."

"Try me."

"I'm not in the mood."

"I wonder if you really know what love is," he said sarcastically, after a while.

"You do?" she asked, just as sarcastically.

"Maybe more than you think."

"You asked me the first time I came down here what had been bothering me. Now I'll tell you."

Paul hesitated for a moment to decide if he should continue. "You remember that night of your father's party?" he began.

"The night you left me?"

"Yes, at the Fourth of July party. I had just returned from an inspection trip near Port Harcourt." He raised himself on his elbow again to face her. "I arrived early

93

at the party, much sooner than when you saw me. I met your father and asked him where you were. He said he thought you might be at the pool."

The words were spewing forth. Paul felt good telling her after all these months of thinking about it. It had a purifying effect.

"I walked to the pool and the place was deserted except for an Englishman. When I told him I was looking for you, he acted very strange. I remember his question vividly: he asked if I were your husband. When I told him no, he seemed more willing to talk, and he told me that you were in the changing room with someone. I couldn't believe it. I had to find out. I was going to storm in on you but I decided instead to wait down the path. After fifteen minutes a black man I had never seen before left you giggling in the pool."

While Paul told his story, and for a short time afterward, his eyes held hers. When he finished, the only sound was that of the rain. Maureen said nothing, but he could see that she understood what he was talking about.

"That's why you walked away?" she asked softly.

He ignored her question. "Was that love?" he asked. "You never said anything."

"There wasn't anything to say, was there? It was all rather obvious."

"And there was no possibility of an explanation?"

"My God, Maureen, you were in there together, in the dark, for more than twenty minutes. What was I to think?"

"I don't know, but you might have at least given me a chance to explain."

"What would Larry have thought if he had been in my place?"

She glared at him, then her eyes filled with tears, but she didn't cry. He had never seen her cry.

"He would have given me a chance to explain. And if it were true, he would have done everything he could to help me find happiness."

"I'm sorry. I guess I'm not that magnanimous."

"I'm sorry, too," Maureen said. She stood up and looked down at him. Her voice trembled with emotion. "Goodbye, Paul." She left the room, and soon he could hear, through the window, her feet splashing through the mud as she ran down the road to the other side of the island.

She had closed the door behind her, and Paul felt that a door had been closed on part of his life. He knew that it was finished between them. For a moment he was overcome by a desire to run after her. He pictured himself catching her in the rain and telling her that he would forget everything if only she would take him back. A crash of thunder and lightning set the room momentarily ablaze with light and shook him from his dream.

CHAPTER XI

Uli, Biafra, December 28, 1969.

When Paul and Moonshine arrived at the plantation in the evening of the next day, Paul was anxious to find a plane leaving the following day for the plateau. But first he wanted to see about getting food for the children in Bugamu. He had promised himself that he would do that, at least, because he couldn't shake the feeling that he was running out on Maureen. Sending food would be a kind of compensation.

Paul used the radio at the plantation to call Fernando Po. He made an agreement with one of the pilots there to fly in the next day and get him out. It would be very expensive, but it was worth it. At that moment Paul would have given all that he had to be back on the plateau. Under the arrangement, the plane would pick him up late the next afternoon at the Uli airstrip which lay a quarter of a mile north of the plantation.

A distant drone could be heard above the cacophony of the people gathered at the narrow piece of tarmac, a straight part of the old highway which served as the airstrip. Children and adults were waiting for the big four-engine DC-6B's and Constellations which would arrive and depart all night long beginning with the coming of darkness. It was too dangerous to fly the relatively slow and lumbering giants during the day. They were no match for the MIG fighters of the federal air force. After one plane was shot down a month ago, the decision had been made to fly only under cover of darkness. Attacks against the airstrip had been sporadic and for the most part ineffective.

Paul spotted the white twin-engine Piper Apache as it cleared the tree tops at the far end of the runway with its flaps down and engines almost idling. The undercarriage of the plane suddenly appeared from the invisible doors under the engine nacelles and in the nose. The plane set down with a slight shriek of tires and trundled quickly toward the end of the runway where Paul stood.

As the plane approached, taxing slowly, Paul still couldn't believe that he would soon be on his way out of this place. He was disturbed that the priest had not shown up yet. Paul had been informed that the Ibo priest, Father Okeke, made all decisions on allocation of food, and that the priest would meet him before he left. Paul hated the idea of leaving without being sure that food would be sent to Bugamu, but he was prepared to do it. He glanced at his watch. There was still time. He knew the pilot would have to refuel.

"Good afternoon."

Paul looked from the approaching plane, a brilliant white in the sunshine, to the shadowed path where the voice came from.

"I am Samuel Okeke," the stranger announced authoritatively as he approached Paul. He was tall, especially for an Ibo, and seen in profile he had a flat face with a broad, flat nose. His jaw jutted slightly forward, and his lips were full. His eyes were most impressive, large, set wide apart, and luminously black. He had a high forehead and wore his thick, dark hair in a moderate Afro style. Paul thought he communicated an unmistakable air of strength, authority and confidence, tempered by a serenity that was revealed in his warm, soft smile. He was obviously a man who could function well under stress. He wore a neat set of olive drab jungle fatigues, with the trousers bloused over his canvas and leather jungle boots. He looked more like a soldier than the priest Paul knew he was.

Paul introduced himself. The priest seemed to recognize his name. They shook hands.

"Where are you going?" Father Okeke asked.

"To the north, but," Paul gestured toward the direction of the river, "my boatman is going to Bugamu and I wanted to try and get some food sent back with him."

The priest looked surprised at first, then smiled. "That is where Maureen Cahill is working." He looked at Paul curiously, as though trying to remember someone he'd met long ago.

"That's right," Paul said with astonishment. "Do you know her?"

"To Miss Cahill I owe my life." Father Okeke spoke slowly and carefully. His speech revealed an accent which sounded like a cross between BBC English and the melodic tones of the Ibo. He seemed young, but Paul had been wrong before about the age of Africans. He reckoned the priest to be in his thirties.

"She saved you life?"

"Of that I am sure," Father Okeke said. "But I am becoming concerned about her now . . ."

"Now that the end is coming." Paul finished the priest's sentence without obvious emotion.

"Yes, we cannot hold out much longer."

"That's why I came back. I tried to convince her to leave, but she won't." Paul shrugged his shoulders.

"You came back?"

"Yes, I was here before. The other day I went up river to talk to her about leaving but she wouldn't listen. She won't leave the children she's caring for. She's rather hysterical on the subject of the children. She's not being reasonable."

"You know, Mr. Jeffries, I have met many people who have come to Biafra to help," Father Okeke said. "Many came at first for money. You would be surprised at the amount of money there is for certain occupations.

"An American helicopter pilot told me yesterday that he saw, from the air, bands of children, two hundred to three hundred strong, roving aimlessly over the countryside. He dropped food and said that watching them fight for it was the most pathetic thing that he had ever seen. He admitted that he had come here for the money, but confessed that if they stopped paying him tomorrow he would continue to fly. I have seen this happen many times, Mr. Jeffries. I cannot explain it, but I am sure that it has to do with being here." He paused. "It could happen to you."

"Not me," Paul said stubbornly. "I'm a business man."

"But you were here, you left, and now you have returned."

"I left for Port Harcourt, but after what I saw there I couldn't just leave. I had to come back and try, at least one more time, to get Miss Cahill out." Paul's eyes traveled to the plane, which had stopped nearby, and returned to meet the priest's eyes. "At one time we were close, but I'm afraid I've failed again."

Father Okeke's eyes lit up and he snapped his fingers. "Of course, Paul Jeffries!" he exclaimed. "She mentioned you to me. You're the man who disappeared."

The priest smiled, and he looked away from Paul to organize his thoughts. "I first met her in Lagos when her father was still ambassador there. I am a priest and I am an Ibo." There was an almost sacred quality about the way he spoke both nouns. "I was traveling the world, trying to solicit support for our cause. I had occasion to go clandestinely into Lagos about six months ago."

"While there, I was introduced to Miss Cahill through a friend. She seemed interested in my work, and she grew sympathetic to the cause of my people. I asked if she would intervene on my behalf with her father, arrange a meeting. God has blessed me with some persuasive powers, Mr. Jeffries, and I was hoping that if I could see the ambassador and explain the position of our people, maybe he could do something to influence the policy of your government in our behalf. Miss Cahill tried, but there was nothing that could be done. I realize now that my dream was based on ignorance. The policy of non intervention had been firmly set in Washington."

Paul was not interested in the politics of the story. "You said she saved your life?" he said impatiently.

"I'm coming to that. About nine months ago I was in in Lagos again. At that time I was and continue to be considered an enemy of the Federal Government. My activities on behalf of my people have made me a fugitive in federal territory. The punishment for treason is . . . ." He left the sentence hanging.

"A firing squad on Bar Beach," Paul supplied.

The priest did not reply, but continued his story.

"One night a few months later I was on the run in Lagos. I had been discovered. Fortunately I was near the American Embassy, and since there was really nowhere else to go, I ran there. The ambassador was having a party that night, I remember. It was the Fourth of July, your Independence Day.

"I avoided the front entrance and went through the embassy grounds to the patio where I tried to lose myself in the party. I found Miss Cahill and told her of my plight. She took me up to the pool, which was very dark, and hid me in one of the changing rooms. She stayed with me, watching, until it was safe to leave. I heard later that federal agents had come to the party as guests to look for me. Thanks to Miss Cahill, I was able to hide until they left."

When the priest finished his story, Paul couldn't speak. He was paralyzed with shock and the dreadful realization that he had misjudged Maureen. His folly was clear to him.

Paul turned from the priest, rubbing the back of his neck, wet with perspriation, with his cold hand. He had to get back to Maureen. He started toward the shadowed path but Father Okeke touched his arm to stop him.

"You say she will not leave?" he asked.

Paul nodded and turned around to face the priest. "I must get there! I've been such a fool!"

"Perhaps there is a way." Father Okeke spoke without excitement, softly and slowly, which annoyed Paul.

"How?"

"You said that she would not leave the children. Then perhaps we can bring the children out. With the children gone, there would not be any reason for her to stay, would there?"

"Brilliant, but how do we do it?" Paul asked eagerly.

"You have a boat. How many children do you think you can bring out at one time in it?"

The idea excited Paul. "I don't know for sure. I'll have to ask Moonshine, but I should think at least a dozen."

"And how many children are there at Bugamu now?"

"I think Maureen said forty, maybe fifty, but no more than fifty."

"That would mean two trips going and coming for each

load of a dozen children," Father Okeke calculated. "It is possible to bring the children here because they have put on more flights, now that they know the final drive is about to begin. Bring the children here, and we can fly them out as long as the airstrip remains open. Once they take it, then we are . . . ." The priest's words trailed off. He didn't want to say what he was thinking.

"A total of eight trips for four loads, or eight days going and coming. Wait a minute!" Paul interrupted himself. "We can cut that time in half! I just remembered that Larry has a boat. With two boats we can be out of there in four days."

"Larry?"

"He's an American medical missionary who's working with Maureen."

"Oh yes, I have heard of him. He is doing a good work." Father Okeke was silent for a moment, lost in his thoughts. "Eight days, I think, would be too long I do not think we can hold out for eight days. But we might very well make it in four days!" He flashed a smile of exuberance and defiance.

"You've got to hold out four more days," Paul demanded.

"Wait a minute! Father Okeke said. There is a piece of canvas covering a stack of large, brown paper bags at the edge of the dock where your boat is. There you will find high protein meal. Take some back with you now and we can take more later.

"What about your plane?" The priest added.

It was apparent to Paul that the pilot, who was surpervising the refueling operation and at the same time casting nervous glances at the setting sun, was ready to go.

"Can you find someone else to go back with him?"

"Of course," the priest said, smiling broadly. "There are so few planes and so many people to go." He made a gesture with his hand to where they were gathering the children for evacuation.

"I'll pay him, you get some other to leave with him."

"Then you are going back to Bugamu now?"

"Yes."

"My words have had an unintended impact on you," the priest said knowingly as Paul started toward the pilot.

CHAPTER XII

Bugamu, Biafra, December 31, 1969.

As they docked at Bugamu, Paul thought he heard the beat of drums. That was strange because the drums had been silent since the night he had first arrived on the island. He impatiently dismissed the sounds as distant thunder and set out for the village as Moonshine tied up the boat.

The main road, covered by a fine, grey dust, was deserted. The putrid smell of rotting fish was in the air, and as he walked the narrow road in the orange-pink glow of sunset, Paul heard the drums again. Their sound was now unmistakable, and it grew louder as he neared the center of the village.

There were only two large structures in the village: Maureen's house, and a one-story wooden frame building with large square openings for windows that had never been placed. The path to Maureen's house led along the side of that building and, as Paul approached it, he noticed yellow glow through the openings. Then he heard singing as well as the rhythmic drumming. He crouched below one of the window spaces and slowly raised his head. Inside, Cherubim and Seraphim cultists were participating in their traditional ceremony. Paul had heard that the cults were active in the Rivers area, but he had never seen them before.

Two drummers, squatting on a small dais, were pounding the "talking" drums with their hands to create a slow, hypnotic beat. The adult men and women of the village, wearing long, white gowns of discarded mosquito netting and carrying lighted tapers, moved in time to the beat around the dirt floor in a half-shuffle, half-procession that eventually formed a large circle. Each man carried a leather pouch which held the small but deadly night adders, thought to bring good fortune if carried through the dance. If the stories were true, Paul knew that the tempo would slowly increase, individual dancers would go into trances, and the evening would end in a wild orgy.

In the center of the circle stood Larry, gesturing wildly and shouting at the "savages" to stop their dance. Then Maureen entered the room from the other door and joined him. She moved to take his hand and lead him from the room, but he pulled away and continued shouting helplessly and flailing his arms in the air.

Paul found the doorway and stood watching almost hypnotized by the sound and the sight. Maureen rushed over to Paul as he entered the room.

"Thank God you're here! You've got to stop him," she said, grabbing Paul's arm and clutching it like a drowning person might hang on to a life preserver. Paul was glad that she was genuinely pleased to see him. He walked to the center of the room and stood at Larry's side. The dancers were as oblivious to his presence as they were to Larry's.

"Larry, come with me," Paul commanded, using his strength to force the young doctor's arms down to his sides. Finally Larry stopped resisting and allowed his arms to go limp. He hung his head in disguest. Paul led him from the floor, out of the candlelit room, onto the village road. Maureen followed them.

"My God, how could they have done it? After all my work," Larry said despondently.

"Relax, Larry. It doesn't matter. We're getting out, all of us," Paul said.

Larry briskly rubbed his arms, as though he were cold. His forehead was wet with perspiration and he continued muttering to himself. Paul's words made no impact on him.

"I've just seen Father Okeke at the plantation. He's thought of the answer to our problems." Paul filled them in as they walked along the narrow alleyway leading to Marueen's house.

"You saw Father Okeke?" Maureen asked. "Oh, Paul, how is he?"

"He's great," Paul answered with enthusiasm.

"You said he has an answer?"

"Two things. First, he confirmed my statement that the end is very near; second, he told me they're putting on extra flights to get as many people out as possible before the airstrip falls. He told me that if we can get the children to Uli, they can be flown to a real hospital on the island of Fernando Po." Paul was pleading his case as usual, like a lawyer before a jury, but this time he was confident that he had a better case than his opponent. "They'll have plenty of food and proper medical care. They've already flown hundreds of children there."

The three walked the rest of the way in silence and entered through the gate in the tall fence that surrounded Maureen's house. Paul was surprised that there was no immediate reaction to his words. Nevertheless, he kept talking.

"I've got a plan," he announced. "With my boat and Larry's, we can evacuate all the kids in four days, or five days at the most. How many children are here?"

"About forty, maybe a few more," Maureen answered. "Larry just brought in some more yesterday."

"Each boat will hold ten to twelve kids, which means two trips with each boat so that we can be out of here in four days."

Sunday greeted them at the door and led them into the living room, then brought in a kerosene lantern.

"I can tell you now that I'm against this plan," Larry said. He had had time to compose himself.

"Why?" Paul shot back.

"You say they are closing the ring, but that ring is around Uli, not around here! I can't imagine federal troops ever coming to this island, but even if they did, they would never harm these children or us."

"You can't be serious," Paul said incredulously. He sat next to Maureen on the couch.

"I'm absolutely serious. Listen, Paul, I know you mean well, but when I came here these people had no medical care and no church. Now the three villages have both. I've — we've — started something and I can't leave now. It's not just me. My family will be joining me soon, and others from our church will follow them."

Larry gestured in the direction of the frenzied dancers. "I realize now that I can't be too impatient. It's going to take time. We're going to have setbacks, but it will only serve to make me, us, concentrate our efforts more."

Larry had turned to face Paul and Maureen as he spoke; his body was a dark silhouette against the glowing red background of the sunset. "I've gone too far to stop now."

"Then you won't help us with your boat?"

"Paul, I need that boat. Without it my whole program would be ineffective. I have to keep making my rounds. If I stop, if I don't double my efforts, they'll all be back doing the juju."

"You're a fool, Larry."

"He who calls his brother a fool is in danger of hell-fire," Larry remarked, returning Paul's glare.

"That's precisely my point. If you stay here you'll burn in the fire that's coming," Paul said bitterly.

"Please, Paul, try to understand my position. I have the greatest respect for you, but I don't think you really understand what we're doing here or how much it means and will mean to these people." Larry looked at Maureen when he finished speaking. He was expecting her support, but she remained silent.

"It's becoming very clear," Paul said soberly.

"Maureen, do you agree? Do you want to leave now?"

"Larry, it's not a question of wanting to leave, but maybe it's the only alternative at this point. At least it's an opportunity that we didn't have before: the chance to get the children to a real hospital and the chance to get ourselves home again. We would all be better off away from here."

"But if we take the children out now, will they ever get to come back to their villages?"

"They're already separated from their parents and their communities," Paul said.

"But they are still close to their ancestral and cultural heritage," Larry insisted.

"They won't have any cultural heritage if they stay," Paul said flatly.

"I'm sorry, I don't agree," Larry said. "Besides, some of these children are too weak to travel." Larry moved away from the window and across the room. He stopped at the kitchen door and waited for Paul to follow him. Paul understood but chose to ignore him. Larry remained there for a moment, looking at both of them in silence, then turned away and left through the kitchen.

Paul got up from the couch and went over to the open French door. He walked onto the small balcony and began to wonder what Maureen must think of him. He had pieced things together during the trip back to Bugamu. He realized then that she had been working for the Ibos even before he met her, that she was a nurse and a devout Catholic. Maybe her religion had had something to do with her commitment. Many Ibos were Catholics and the Catholic church, through Caritas, had been one of the few international organizations which were actively helping them.

Maureen had probably been acting as some kind of courier when they first saw each other that night on the road, Paul realized. He had to laugh when he remembered that he had gotten a federal officer to take her back through the roadblocks into the city, when she had, most likely, been acting on behalf of the Ibos. He amused himself by wondering how the Minister of Communications would react if he knew that his American colleague was helping the Ibos.

There was no moon, and the clouds had floated away. Paul located the Southern Cross. Away from the city lights the stars shown brilliantly against the black sky.

"Paul," Marueen said from inside. "What are you doing?"

"Just enjoying the night. The stars are stunning."

"I often come out here at night when I'm alone and the skies are clear," she said, joining him on the balcony. "I love to look at the stars. I wish I knew them all by name."

"Why didn't you tell me Samuel Okeke was a priest and that you were hiding him from the police that night at your father's party?" Paul asked without looking at her.

The silence of the night was occasionally broken by the sounds of katydids on the river banks. The fragrance of the frangipanis that grew next to the fence graced the night air.

"I don't really know," she said softly. "So much had happened, I guess I just didn't want to talk about it. After the war, maybe it seemed a little petty." Her voice broke and she took a minute to compose herself.

"Maybe I felt it was too important to you. I guess I didn't want it to be that important to you," she said.

"What could be more important to me?"

"I don't mean it that way. When I finally found out what was bothering you, when you told me the other day, I became upset and then angry. I thought that if you could believe that, then maybe I didn't know you very well.

A gentle breeze was stirring. The night was uncommonly cool for the time of year. Paul wanted to warm Maureen in his arms.

"You've been working with the Ibos all along, haven't you?"

"For a while."

"When did it start?"

She was silent for a while before speaking.

"After we were at the embassy in Lagos for some time, I began to see what was happening in the country. I met a few attractive, intelligent people, many of whom had been educated in the States, who couldn't understand how the U.S. could stand by and do nothing." She spoke softly and slowly. Melancholy characterized her voice.

"I think the most unpleasant experience in my life was when we were in Lagos. When I understood what was going on, I tried to get my father to persuade the U.S. government to become involved here, to do something before the Ibos were decimated. He was sympathetic but said there was nothing he could do."

"So there I was, part of my country's policy of non intervention, living in ambassadorial luxury while others were here risking their lives, working to help save the Ibos. I finally knew that I had to do something."

"Why didn't you tell me what you were up to?"

"What would you have done? What difference would it have made?"

"I don't know what I would have done, but I might have done things differently."

"With you working for the federal government, like my father, and me working for the Ibos?"

"I should have known. Now I know why you were so upset when you visited me in Jos, when we went into town and you saw the refugee children."

"It was like being in Lagos again. Living in luxury at Hill Station, while the people whose country this is were suffering and dying."

"That's why you left?"

"Yes. I couldn't stay there."

"Like me."

"Oh, Paul, I didn't expect you to take up the Ibo cause. I realize that not everyone believes in the same thing; not everyone believes in anything. At first I though you were *against* the Ibos because you were working for the federal government. I didn't know how much I could tell you. But I know differently now. I understand your work is very important to the future of this country."

"The future . . .," he mused.

"What?"

"We work for the future of things — a country, a people, technology, satellites. But the really important future is in ourselves. If we could only work that hard and plan that far in advance for our own futures, maybe we would be happier."

"Have you ever been happy, Paul?"

"I was happy once."

"When?"

"When we were together on the plateau," he said without looking at her.

She put her hands on the balcony railing and leaned forward. "Perhaps you can't look for happiness; it has to find you."

He looked at her then and asked, "What about you?"

"I'm happy now," she said.

"Why?"

"The night air, the stars, and . . . ."

"And?"

She looked at him and smiled the smile he remembered most.

"You!"

And then she was in his arms.

CHAPTER XIII

Bugamu, Biafra, January 1, 1970.

The sound of a motor sputtering, stopping, and catching again startled Paul. He stirred in his makeshift bed under the tin roof of the boat. Then he recognized the noise as an outboard engine. He lifted the netting which, in a rather futile attempt at comfort, had been hastily rigged in the darkness the night before. Now the other pirogue, which had been tied along the opposite side of the dock, was gliding silently out toward midstream. The motor caught again.

Paul was wide awake now and quickly crawled out from under the roof. He stood in his shorts, watching the boat moving more swiftly downstream. Larry was seated in the shadow under the roof of the boat looking determinedly in the direction his boatman was steering.

"Larry, come back! We need that boat. We can all be out of here in two days!" Paul was sure that Larry had heard him shout but no response came from the boat. He watched the pirogue as it moved farther away, the sound of its motor fading, the boat growing smaller. When it had disappeared from view, Paul turned to face the island. He made a silent vow that he would never forgive Larry for this. The fact that they had silently pushed off from the dock, not starting the motor until mid-stream was, to Paul, a sneaking away which only strengthened his condemnation of Larry.

To hell with him, Paul thought. We'll make it without him. He can stay here until the end; that's his problem. At least he would stay alone. Paul had persuaded Maureen to leave and that was to him a personal victory over Larry. He relished his triumph.

But Paul was still frustrated from the night before. After Larry had left them together at her house, after their reconciliation, Paul had wanted to stay the night. Maureen had resisted. She couldn't sleep with him now, she said, not while Larry was just across the island. She needed time. They had waited this long and she asked Paul to be patient a while longer. He had grabbed a mosquito net and stormed out of her house, and slept in the boat.

Now he hastily dressed in the early morning light and set out for the clinic. He was determined to have it out with Maureen. When he arrived, he was surprised to find only Sunday and the children.

"Where is madam, Sunday?" Paul queried the houseboy who was looking after the children.

Sunday approached the table in the middle of the room near where Paul was standing. He raised his hands palms upward in a gesture of helplessness and tears welled up in his eyes.

"Madam see paper," Sunday said, pointing to a crumpled sheet of paper on the table and then running his fingers down his face as if to imitate tears. "She cry and go back home."

114

Paul picked up the wad of paper, carefully unwrapped it and read the note. It was in Larry's almost childlike handwriting:

Maureen Dearest:

    I realized last night that you have made the decision to leave Bugamu. With your leaving with the children, there is no reason for me to stay on. I shall concentrate my efforts on my other two villages. Your leaving forces me to change my plans. The adjustment will be difficult. I will miss you.

Love,

Larry

The words and her reaction to them infuriated Paul. He stood holding the note for a moment, then balled it up again with one hand and turned to the open doorway. A sudden urge to go to her swept him. Larry still had a hold on her and Paul was tired of trying to compete with him.

With all of his strength he suddenly hurled the balled-up note against the wall. The wad of paper bounced off the wall and landed harmlessly on a little girl, not more than four, who raised her hands in fear and began crying. Paul's attention was suddenly riveted on her. Instantly he felt guilty that he had caused her such distress. He stood in the middle of the room for a second longer and took another look out the open door in the direction of Maureen's house. Then he turned back to the child. He had often felt abhorrence at the sight of these children and had avoided their hollow stares. Usually he could readily turn away; either Larry or Maureen was there to tend to them. Paul took a second to appraise the child. She continued her wailing. He squatted down in front of her, lifted her into his arms, and stood up. He was surprised that she was so light and that his touch seemed to calm her. He called to Sunday.

115

"You bring that other child that can't walk. We go for the boat."

"Some pickin' walk with us," Sunday said.

"Yes, some can follow, but we can only take ten this time."

Sunday immediately began to give instructions in the vernacular to those children who would walk with them. Just as he was leaving the room with the girl in his arms, Paul spotted Hyacinth standing in a corner and looking terrified.

"You take care of the others that we leave, Hyacinth. I will come back for you."

Wide-eyed, the boy nodded and then returned Paul's smile. As Paul walked, holding the child, the old abhorrence disappeared. He held her close, and when they arrived at the boat she was asleep in his arms.

Pewter-colored clouds, low and heavy caressed the tops of the mangrove trees. Rain had been falling intermittently all afternoon as Paul and Moonshine made their way back to Bugamu. They had delivered the first load of children to the plantation yesterday. Now Paul hoped they could reach Bugamu before the rain came steadily.

As they neared the village he could see a lone figure on the dock. It could only be Maureen, he knew. Her waiting like that both excited and distressed him. He would have been happier had he known with certainty that it was him she was waiting for, but it could also be Larry. From far off both boats appeared alike.

What distressed Paul even more was the knowledge that Colonal Barka and his men would approach the village in the same way. If she were standing on the dock like that and Barka should appear, by the time she discovered her mistake it would be too late. Paul couldn't take his eyes off her as they closed the last one hundred yards.

She appeared so vulnerable. Seeing her reassured him that Barka and his men had not yet visited the island.

"Any word of Larry?" Paul asked wearily as he climbed up onto the dock. He still harbored a secret hope that the young missionary would return with the other boat. The thought of the six days on the river that lay ahead for him left Paul totally enervated.

"No," she said, sensing his exhaustion.

"You know, Maureen," he scolded as he stood up and faced her after lashing the bow line to the dock, "you shouldn't stand out here like that when a boat approaches from the distance. It could be Colonel Barka."

"I knew it was you."

"How?" Paul's voice took on a tone of frustration and disbelief. "Larry's got a boat just like it."

"I *knew* it was you," she said softly but with conviction.

Heavy drops of rain struck them just then.

"How long have you been waiting?" he asked, really looking at her for the first time since he arrived. Her hair was damp and had taken on a darker color so that it appeared almost brown. Little drops of water formed crystal beads on her face and lips. Her blue cotton blouse and blue denim shorts were wet.

"You're soaked," Paul said.

She pushed back her thick hair with a graceful movement of her right hand and smiled, but didn't speak.

"I've made supper for you and Moonshine. I asked Sunday to take Moonshine's supper to the clinic. I thought they could eat there and then stay there tonight. We can eat at my place."

Paul nodded agreement and turned to his boatman. He gave Moonshine instructions for preparations for the next day's trip.

Maureen and Paul walked without speaking toward her house. He could sense a change in her but wasn't sure what it meant.

"The first load of children is in the hospital now on Fernando Po," he said, breaking the silence.

"So soon!" she cried with genuine surprise and joy.

"It doesn't take long, once we get them to the plantation. So long as they hold out there, they'll keep flying the evacuation missions."

"Oh, Paul, it makes me so happy to know that they are there already! Somehow I really didn't believe it was possible. Now you've proved it; I was wrong *and* Larry was wrong. I know now we made the right decision."

He was glad that she was happy but he was too tired to show much emotion. All he could think about now was the river. Whenever he closed his eyes, he could see the river moving toward him. He wasn't even hungry. All he wanted then was sleep. But he was also afraid. Lately while on the river he had found himself looking over his shoulder more often. The image of Colonel Barka and his men was part of his vision of the river. He could see the boatload of men bristling with guns pursuing him constantly. He pictured them arriving at the island while he was away.

When they arrived at the house Maureen put the finishing touches on their supper while he walked out onto the balcony. The great Niger River lay below, strong brown god, someone had called it. It appeared almost black now as the sky had darkened with the rain clouds and the coming of the brief African twilight, soon to be followed by darkness. His eyes followed the course of the river in the direction that he had come. He searched the dark waters for any signs of a boat.

"Paul."

"I'm out here on the balcony."

"It's raining."

"I don't care, I'm already wet."

"What is it?"

"I wanted to see what kind of a lookout point you had from here."

"What?" she repeated, coming out to join him. She stood next to him on the narrow balcony. The rain was mistlike but warm. It tasted sweet on his lips. He was silent as he stared in the direction from which he had come an hour earlier.

"You see that?" he asked with a haggard note in his voice. Her eyes followed the direction of his stare. "That's where he'll come from."

"Who?"

"Barka," he said flatly.

The bend in the river far downstream was barely visible in the rain and dimming light. Paul wondered if even in good weather one could see a boat from this distance. He knew the house could be seen from there and would attract Barka. He wished he had binoculars and made a mental note to get a pair for her when he was next at the plantation. He looked from the river to the woman at his side. Her face revealed puzzlement.

"Colonel Barka and his men will come. I know it. I can feel it. And when he comes, he'll come from the same direction that I come from when I return from the plantation," Paul said, shifting his glance from her to the river again.

She didn't speak but her eyes searched his face.

"From now on when you go to the clinic across the island, have Sunday stay up here and stand guard. If he sees a boat — any boat — he's to go to you and you both must take to the bush." Paul spoke without taking his eyes off the river.

"What about the children?"

"They'll be all right. Barka won't hurt the children," Paul lied, remembering that some children had been slaughtered in the Port Harcourt raid.

There was a short, heavy silence.

"If you were both over there at the clinic, you wouldn't even know his boat had arrived. They could march right up on you," he continued.

"But I need Sunday to help me there," she said at last.

"Listen," Paul said, grabbing both of her arms, his voice cracking, "there are some men out on that river now who have raped and murdered nuns at a hospital in Port Harcourt. Each day that passes, each new defeat for Biafra brings them closer to this island. You've still got some childish belief that he won't harm you, but you're wrong. You're dead wrong."

She was staring at him wide-eyed, shocked at his emotion and the pain in her arms from his vice-like grip.

Then, just as suddenly, Paul released her. He turned in frustration, entering the room and leaving her on the balcony. He stood with his back to her. In a moment he felt her beside him, her touch on his arm like a caress.

"Paul, please take off those wet clothes, you'll catch cold. You can put on my robe," she said, ignoring his outburst. She disappeared into her bedroom, returning almost immediately with the robe in her hand. "You can change in here," she said, leading him into the other bedroom.

"I'm sorry I yelled at you."

"There's something I want to show you," she said and left him alone in the room still lit by the dying light from the window.

Paul took off his wet clothes in silence and put on the terry cloth robe. He looked at himself in the mirror on the bureau, the only other piece of furniture in the room other than the bed. He was satisfied that the gown was sufficiently unisex so that he could appear in it.

He returned to the living room. The wind had picked up and now the rain was blowing into the room through the still-open French doors. He took one last look at the river blending into the blackness below and closed the doors. He crossed the room to the couch where he sat down, putting his feet up on the coffee table. For the first time in a long while he began to relax. He sat there watching the light fade from the room. He wasn't so tired now. It was quiet except for rain against the windows.

The bedroom door opened slowly, almost hesitantly. Light was pouring out from behind it. He turned just as Maureen appeared. She was wearing a floor-length ivory colored dress with long sleeves and she was holding the Kerosene lamp. He was mesmerized by the vision. She approached him and set the lamp on the coffee table. Then she stepped back so he could get a better view. He was speechless. The soft lamplight washed away her slight tired look; it brought out the gold color of her hair. Her eyes sparkled and she was smiling.

"Do you like it?" she asked.

"You look radiant," he said, standing up. "The dress . . ."

"It's my wedding gown. It was my mother's. We brought it with us to the embassy. Somehow I must have put it in with my things. When I discovered that I had it. I wanted to send it back, but there was no way."

"It's beautiful."

"I couldn't button the back," she said, turning slightly and revealing her naked back.

"In such a gown you should be married in a cathedral with a great organ playing and with flower girls," Paul said, unable to look away from her.

"Where is not so important."

"No, I suppose not."

"If you love someone, it doesn't matter where."

"No." His voice cracked. "Perhaps if I hadn't been such a fool it would have been different."

"Do you love me, Paul?" she asked, breaking a long silence in which only their eyes communicated.

"How can you ask? You know I do, with all my heart."

"This should be our wedding night, Paul."

CHAPTER XIV

Bugamu, Biafra, January 8, 1970.

A little over a wcck had passed since Paul had returned to Maureen. Larry had not come back to the island. The evacuation process with just the one boat was more diffi-cult than Paul had imagined. The eight days that he had calculated as adequate for the evacuation of all the child-ren with just one boat had been over optimistic. There were delays caused by mechanical problems, and the fact that his piroque was just not large enough to carry ten children when some were on stretchers. But Father Okeke's reckoning that the airstrip at Uli could not last longer than eight days had been equally pessimistic. They were still holding out. He and Moonshine were on the river between Bugamu and the plantation almost all the time. Paul was only able to spend every other night with Maureen.

This last trip he had had the opportunity to speak with Father Okeke. Paul told him of his "marriage" to Maureen and asked his advice. Father Okeke congratulated him and explained that according to his religion, a man and woman marry each other and the priest only officiates. But he offered to perform a ceremony when Paul and Maureen arrived at the plantation.

Paul was anxious to tell Maureen the news. He knew that she would be thrilled by the idea. She had agreed to an extended honeymoon on the plateau. During his days on the river and nights at the plantation, away from her, his mind was filled with her. He relived each moment they had spent together, and he loved the thought that she would be waiting for him when he went back. What it meant to love someone in that way! He wouldn't have felt it was possible before, but now his life had new meaning. The knowledge that the next trip would be the last one and that she would be on it filled him with joy.

Paul still resented Larry for not having helped him. If he had they would have been out of there sooner. But when Paul had verbalized his resentment to Maureen, she pleaded Larry's case and asked Paul to try to convince him to leave with them if and when he next saw him. Time was running short. Upon each return, Paul brought news of the latest disaster for the Ibos. Maureen was now convinced that she had made the correct decision and that there was no alternative to leaving. Paul prayed that the airstrip could hold out a few days more.

The river had widened again, and Paul looked ahead for the first signs of Bugamu. As he trained his eyes on the bank of mangrove far ahead, he somehow sensed that something was wrong. The pirogue was moving agonizingly slowly. He checked the known landmarks to be sure that he was not disoriented and glanced back at Moonshine who was shaking his head in confusion and fright. As they rounded the bend, the village came into clear view.

Paul found the sight incredible and horrifying. The large building that had served as Maureen's house and had been a beacon during all these river trips was no longer there. He blinked to be sure his eyes weren't deceiving him, but there was no doubt.

"Madam house finished," Moonshine shouted.

"As they neared the dock, Paul quickly surveyed the rest of the village. Everything else appeared normal. He leapt from the boat onto the landing and set off at a dead run toward where Maureen's house had stood. When he left the main road to take the narrower path which led to her house, he smelled smoke. He couldn't see any, but the odor was unmistakable.

He passed the last group of huts that blocked his view, and what he saw made him feel as though he had been bashed in the stomach. The house was nothing but a smouldering heap of rubble. He passed through the open gate of the iron fence, which was still standing, and stood before the ruins in shock. After a few seconds of what seemed to him to be total numbness, he dashed toward the smoking debris and began to claw madly through it, unmindful of the glowing embers which singed his hands and arms.

Then, stymied by some huge beams and blocks of cement, he ran toward the clinic, frantic and desperate. Oh, God, if only Larry is here, together we can dig her out, he thought. Sweat was flooding down from his forehead, into his eyes and mouth, as he ran through the hot staleness of the dusk. The clinic buildings were still visible against the darkening sky. He shouted for Larry. The front door of the main building swung open, and Larry's tall figure filled the entranceway.

"Paul!"

"My God, Larry, what's happened?" Paul shouted, out of breath, as he closed the last few yards separating him from the young doctor.

"They bombed her house," Larry whispered.

"What about Maureen? Where is she? I couldn't find her.!"

"She's inside."

Paul moved to enter the clinic when Larry stopped him.

"There wasn't much I could do." His voice was drained and he was trembling.

Paul pushed past Larry and sprinted into the main room. It smelled of the sick children who were still there, but Maureen wasn't among them. As he scoured the room for her, candlelight from the adjoining room, where he had slept the night of his second visit, caught his attention. He stuck his head in the open doorway, then stepped timidly inside, fearful of what he might see.

She was on Larry's bed, surrounded by the mosquito netting. What appeared to be a makeshift wire frame had been rigged over her bed and a sheet draped over it so that it covered her body to her shoulders but did not touch her. Her eyes, which were closed when Paul entered the room, opened when he stopped at the foot of the bed. He had never seen them look so bright. She smiled and raised her left hand to gesture hello, then patted the bed weakly, indicating that he should sit there. He gently lifted the netting over him and carefully sat on the edge of the bed.

The color of her face was not much different from the white sheet that covered her. Paul bent over and softly kissed her on the lips. As he sat up, she managed a faint smile, and her left hand touched his. He wanted to say something, to do something to make her more comfortable, but there was nothing he could say or do. He gently touched her cold forehead and she closed her eyes. In a short while she was asleep.

Paul rose from the bed and stood at her feet, wondering if he should snuff out the candles. He finally did not and tiptoed out of the room and out of the clinic. He stopped outside the doorway, a few feet from where Larry was still standing.

"What happened to her?" Paul spoke sharply, out of desperation.

"Her place was bombed last night. I was in Andonni. We were hit too, so I came here. When I got back this morning, I found her among the ruins." Larry spoke without expression, looking off into the distance.

"How bad is she?"

"Burns."

"Napalm," Paul said. "They used napalm on the village."

"Not only does she have third-degree burns over more than 18 percent of her body, but she's suffered respiratory damage from inhaling the hot gases. People with her degree of burns, and covering that much of the body, don't normally survive," Larry continued clinically, more to himself than to Paul.

"She's not an ordinary person," Paul said. "She'll survive. Ordinary persons don't do the things she has done."

"You don't understand, Paul. No one with injuries like that . . . ." Larry's voice trailed off as he faced Paul at last.

"I don't want to hear that, Larry!" Paul shouted. "If she dies . . . ."

They didn't speak for a few minutes. Then Paul said decisively, "We've got to get her out of here tomorrow, at first light. We'll take her to the plantation in my boat. You can bring the other children in your boat."

"I can't," Larry said quickly.

"Why not?" Paul asked quietly. He was trying to control the anger and recrimination that he had long felt for Larry.

"My boatman has fled," Larry announced. "When I found Maureen I ran to the dock to get him to help me carry her to the clinic, but he was gone with the boat."

"That's just great!" Paul snapped. He thought for a moment before speaking again, then forced the words out. "We'll just have to leave some kids behind. I'm taking her out of here tomorrow morning. And I want you to be here. She may need you."

"I'll be here," Larry promised. And he walked away, into the night.

CHAPTER XV

Uli, Biafra, January 11, 1970.

They stood on the edge of the jungle in the night, waiting for what everyone knew, but no one would admit, would be the last plane. The airport was going to fall before the next dawn. Their vigil had been a long one, and they were all very tired for they had spent the day bringing the children down from the plantation for the flight. The last trip from Bugamu had been the saddest experience of Paul's life. They had set off early that morning to avoid the heat that was sure to come. Maureen's stretcher was rigged under the roof of the boat to protect her from the sun and the rain. There was room aboard for a few more children, but half a dozen others had to be left behind, alone, with Sunday.

Maureen had been conscious then, and she protested with all her ebbing strength, especially when it was discovered that in the excitement Hyacinth had been left behind with the others. She lost a lot of strength during the trip and was exhausted, yet, at times she seemed euphoric, due no doubt to the morphine injections Larry was administering. She never complained about her pain, and for most of the journey she was at peace in a blessed, deep sleep.

Once she had asked Paul if he had told Father Okeke about their marriage. When he said that the priest was pleased and wanted to perform a ceremony at the plantation, the news cheered her. Larry never left her side except when one of the children had a problem that Paul couldn't handle.

As soon as they arrived at the plantation in the early evening, Maureen was rushed to the aid station run by a volunteer medical team from Sweden. The young doctor who headed the team interrupted his work preparing the children for evacuation to devote his energies exclusively to Maureen. Father Okeke was also there. His presence buoyed Maureen and he administered the last rites of his church to her.

While the Swedish doctor and Larry attended to Maureen and then to those others who required medical aid, Paul helped to transport the prepared children down to the airstrip. The Swedish doctor had chosen only those children who were most likely to survive, and they were placed atop a large flatbed trailer that had to be pushed by hand along the quarter-mile road that cut through the forest of rubber trees to the landing strip. The labor exhausted Paul, but he welcomed the distraction that the work offered.

When he and the other transporters returned to the aid station after five trips, Maureen was ready to go with the last group of evacuees. The doctors had done all that could be done medically for her, and the prognosis was frankly pessimistic. The linen on her stretcher had been changed, and intravenous feeding equipment had been rigged onto a small pole attached to the side of the stretcher. Paul and

Larry loaded her onto the cart, along with the others, and set off down the road. When they arrived at the airstrip there was nothing to do but wait.

Paul wouldn't leave her side now, not until she was on the plane — but what if it didn't come! He wouldn't dwell on that possibility. He cast a nervous glance at the black sky. The darkness now offered hope, for with the dawn no more planes would come. Just then he was aware of a strange silence. The sounds of the approaching war had momentarily ceased. The odd peacefulness affected everyone. It was an ominous but welcome respite.

Maureen opened her eyes to Paul who was standing at her side, still holding her hand and looking toward the silent blackness at the edge of the runway.

"Paul," she said softly.

He bent down toward her.

"Would you ask Father Okeke to perform the ceremony." Paul had forgotten that he had mentioned it to her.

"It's too much for you now. You need rest," Paul replied, touching her cold forehead.

"No, Paul, it's important to me. I want our marriage sanctified. I want Larry to be here too. He can be a witness."

Father Okeke, seeing her talking to Paul, joined them.

"Father," Paul said relieved that the priest was there, "she wants you to marry us now. It's important to her . . .to us."

The priest's eyes met Maureen's and held them for a moment.

She nodded. Father Okeke moved to stand next to her. He took her hand in his.

"Maureen, you wish to be married now to Paul?"

"Yes, father," she said.

Larry, who had never been far from Maureen, had also noticed that she was conscious and approached them.

"We need you to be a witness at the wedding of Maureen and Paul." The priest spoke the words solemnly.

"Of course, father," Larry said, smiling at Maureen who returned his smile.

The priest took Paul's hand and placed it in Maureen's. He pressed their hands together for a long moment in silence.

"Paul and Maureen, my dear friends," he began, "you have asked me to be a witness at your marriage. You wish to express your love by this union." Just then the momentary quiet was ended by the thunder of incoming 122 mm. rockets which were now impacting in the rubber trees about a quarter of a mile away from the runway.

"Do you, Maureen, take Paul as your husband, to love throughout your life, forsaking all others?" The priest was rushing now and extemporizing.

"I do," Maureen said, and she smiled, looking at Paul.

"Do you, Paul, take Maureen as your wife, to love throughtout your life, forsaking all others?"

"I do," Paul said. He felt Maureen squeeze his hand.

"You are man and wife."

Larry leaned over and kissed Maureen and then he rushed away to tend to the group of children and evacuees who were crowding together now as the violence approached them with renewed strength. The priest also left them.

"Paul, promise me something."

"Anything." He could see that her strength was fading. "You should try to sleep."

"I will soon, but first promise me that you'll help Larry. He needs your help."

For an instant the words stuck in his throat. "I promise."

His words relieved her. Her breathing had slowed; her body relaxed now and she was in a deep sleep, oblivious to the renewed sounds of war.

Paul continued to hold her cold hand, wishing desperately that he could transmit his strength to her. He thanked God for letting her sleep. He watched Larry crouching next to an unconscious child on a stretcher not far away. Their eyes met for an instant. They did not speak, and Larry returned his attention to the child.

Soon the rumble of federal artillery grew louder, sounding like a huge, menacing beast creeping up on them in the jungle. Then mortar rounds began slamming into the canopy of rubber trees that surrounded them. Occasionally Paul could hear the staccato bark of automatic weapons in the distance. The relief workers had gathered around the children to protect them. Many more refugees streamed onto the airfield, hoping to be taken away when the plane came. No one would tell them that there would be no room.

Suddenly a mortar round exploded in a bright flash, just to the side of the runway. Paul threw his arms over Maureen, and everyone else fell to the ground. The small arms fire was growing louder as the distant sound of airplane engines could first be heard. Before the plane appeared, rebel soldiers came scurrying out of the trees and charged past the refugees. The soldiers shouted and gesticulated wildly toward the direction they were coming from and ran for the safety of the bush on the other side of the airstrip.

Just as they disappeared, the whole area was bathed in the landing lights of the large DC-6B plane coming over the tree tops. The makeshift runway lights were turned on shortly before the plane touched down on the tarmac. Its tires screeched and smoked, and the aircraft careened in a thumping, bouncing roll to the far end of the runway.

The plane slowed but did not stop, then turned around extraordinarily quickly. The runway lights were doused as the plane began to trundle back to where the small band of people were gathered. The huge door at the rear of the fuselage swung open as it approached, and a small, metal ladder slid out and down to the tarmac. Paul could see the flight crew chief standing in the doorway. He appeared like a ghost in the dim, blue-green light emanating from the ship. Paul and Larry pushed the cart quickly forward to meet the taxiing plane.

"Relief personnel on first! We will hand the injured up to them," Father Okeke shouted, trying to make himself heard above the noise of the four idling engines and the whistling propellers. The relief workers hurried to the fuselage and, one by one, climbed up the ladder and were helped into the aircraft by the crew chief. Paul and Larry stood behind the children, many of whom couldn't climb the ladder and had to be handed into the waiting arms of the relief workers.

Maureen was the last to be put aboard. When all the children had been boarded, Paul jumped onto the cart, parked just below the gaping cargo doorway. Each took an end of the stretcher and slowly lifted it into the plane. The jarring movement brought her back to conciousness. She opened her eyes, looked at Paul and smiled weakly.

Maureen was no sooner on the plane than another mortar round slammed into the runway not far from the plane. Paul was quick to duck but he felt the heat and shock of the blast against his face, followed by an acrid smell and the sound of shrapnel rattling against the fuselage like rain on a tin roof. The plane's four powerful radial engines were gunned and the aircraft shuddered as the pilot pumped the brakes. Larry and the crew chief stood in the doorway across from Paul on the flatbed. The crew chief reached to pick up the ladder and pull it into the plane. Paul could see the chief's lips move as he spoke into his headset, instructing the pilot to take off.

Larry suddenly jumped onto the cart next to Paul. "Stay with her!" Paul shouted at Larry. His words were a harsh command. It was the only time he had spoken to Larry since they arrived at the plantation.

"You're her husband, you should be with her now," Larry retorted.

"She doesn't need a husband now, she needs a doctor. When she's awake she'll want to know about Hyacinth and the other children at Bugamu." Paul still had to shout to be heard above the noise of the engines but he found that shouting offered him a strange kind of therapy, a release from his anger and frustration. "Tell her that I got them out okay and that I'll join her on Fernando Po soon."

Larry nodded almost submissively. His eyes met Paul's icy glare and then he turned to reach for the crew chief's outstretched hand. He was lifted aboard just as the plane started to move forward and, at once, a crescendo of small arms fire rang out over the plane's racket. Two more mortar rounds hit the runway. The engines roared, the cargo door slammed shut and the plane lurched ahead. Paul turned his back on the slip-stream, hunched his shoulders and put his hand to his face to shield his eyes from the storm of dust and debris being kicked up by the taxiing plane.

When he opened his eyes again he saw Father Okeke standing at the edge of the runway, shouting for Paul to follow him. Paul jumped from the cart and followed the priest. They reached the far side of the clearing in time to watch the plane turn around quickly, flashing its landing lights. The runway lights did not respond. With a deafening roar, the aircraft shuddered and rumbled and slowly picked up speed.

135

Paul was fascinated with the scene and the noise as the huge plane ran past them with its exhaust pipes spewing red and purple fire. The plane lifted off the ground. In the glow of the lights, Paul saw the landing gear fold into the aircraft just as it barely cleared the clump of trees at the end of the landing strip.

Paul and Father Okeke started to run through the darkness along the road back to the plantation compound.

"Where will you go now, Paul?" the priest yelled as they ran.

"I'm going back to Bugamu, father. What about you?"

"I have a place where I will be safe. But you must hurry before the government troops get here!"

They were running hard and fast. The quarter-mile run was exhausting in the muggy night heat and Paul felt a sharp pain growing in his side. When they reached the house, which was still lighted by the lamp Paul had left burning, they both stopped to catch their breath, and Father Okeke grabbed Paul's hand.

"Good luck, my friend. You must leave now. I hope to see you again in better times. When all this is over, come back to my country."

The words sounded strange to Paul. He wondered what they meant, but there was no time to ask.

"Thank you, father, for everything. Good luck to you."

They shook hands one last time in the traditional Ibo handclasp that ended with a snap of the fingers.

"About Maureen," the priest said, "You did the right thing.." "You must hurry now," Father Okeke shouted, pushing Paul toward the river bank.

Paul sprinted across the lawn toward the light coming from the torch on the boat. He heard shouts and looked over his shoulder to see federal soldiers running riot around the plantation compound. Just as he reached the dock, an automatic weapon opened up behind him.

He heard bullets whistling past him and over his head as he leaped into the boat.

Moonshine was trying frantically to start the boat's motor. Paul was almost glad that the boatman hadn't been able to get it going because he wasn't certain that Moonshine would have waited for him if the engine had caught. Paul snapped the bowline from the dock and pushed off. He crawled to the middle of the boat and grabbed Moonshine's torch to turn it off. Just then Moonshine gave the engine cord a mighty jerk, and the motor started. He immediately pointed the bow downstream, and the boat glided through the water, slowly at first, gradually picking up speed as it reached midstream.

Motor rounds were still exploding near the plantation compound, illuninating the river ahead. Paul thought he could hear armored vehicles moving across the plantation and he knew then that the only escape from Bugamu now was by sea. He wondered, as they rounded the first bend in the river that put the action behind them, if Father Okeke had made it safely to his sanctuary.

CHAPTER XVI

Between Uli and Bugamu, Biafra, January 12, 1970.

The river was still wide where they moored the boat for the night along a grassy bank. Here the sounds of the battle faded into the sounds of the jungle. Paul tried to sleep, but couldn't. Rain had started falling shortly after they fled Uli, and the accompanying thunder kept him from what he knew would be a fitful sleep.

"Moonshine! Moonshine!" Paul spoke urgently as he shook his boatman awake. "It's morning, Moonshine!"

By the time Moonshine sat up and put on his tattered tennis shoes and dirty sweatshirt, the darkness had been replaced by a soft grey light. Paul glanced at the yellow sky still covered with low clouds. The morning air was heavy and sweet-smelling. Moonshine crawled back to the engine and Paul climbed forward to the bow, which was nudging the bank, and jumped into the grass-covered mud. He stretched his body awake before unlooping the bowline from around the trunk of the mimosa tree that stood near the water's edge.

Moonshine had gotten the engine started before Paul leaped back into the boat. He sat under the tin roof while Moonshine steered the boat toward the middle of the stream, then navigated the craft downstream toward the river.

They passed what had once been the village of Andonni in the late afternoon. All that remained of the village was a blackened, open area of smouldering rubble where huts had once stood. Paul looked at Moonshine who gaped in horror at the ruins, making a wide berth of the dead village by keeping the boat close to the far bank.

"Andonni finish'," Moonshine muttered.

Moonshine looked at Paul who made a motion with his hand in the air, indicating that airplanes had caused the destruction.

"*Baburdan*," Moonshine exclaimed, flaying his arms. "Bring fire, bring palavar, plenty, too much, too much trouble."

Paul nodded and looked back toward the desolate patch on the bank as they passed under the shade of the mangrove. Moonshine said nothing more for a long time, but occasionally he looked over his shoulder for a glimpse of the village which could no longer be seen. The sun sat low in the evening sky and the river flowed in the shadow of the banks. Paul expected Bugamu to open up on them around every bend of the river.

As he strained to see in the distance, he couldn't shake the mental picture of Maureen waiting for him on the tiny landing. He couldn't imagine the island without her. The last few trips there had filled him with the anticipation of seeing her and the excitement that came when her house appeared from way down river. The house had become a welcoming beacon.

But she was gone. The house was gone. The island had become a place of pain. Paul knew that he would probably

139

never return there after this trip, unless she got well. He half-smiled as he envisioned the two of them going back as tourists. Then he remembered how she looked when he had put her on the plane, asleep and so white. He had to keep hoping for her recovery. He figured that they would have arrived at Fernando Po the night before, and that she could be on her way to a hospital in the States. Even though he blamed Larry for much of what had happened to her, knowing that he had flown out with her gave Paul some comfort.

They passed the junction where the smell of the sea was strong, and Paul longed again for the open water and the fresh, salt breeze.

"*Kai*," Moonshine shouted.

Paul looked back to the boatman, who was pointing ahead.

"*Huba*."

Paul strained his eyes in the fading light to look in the direction that Moonshine was indicating. Then he saw the darker open patch against the bank ahead. Bugamu had been destroyed by fire in the same fashion as Andonni.

They tied the boat to a charred pole sticking out of the water near a crumpled pile of wood that had been the dock.

"Come with me to the hospital, Moonshine," Paul instructed. They followed the narrow road that led between the mass of smouldering wood and twisted corrugated iron roofs that once had been the marketplace.

It was dark, but a bright moon lit the devasted village with a soft, silvery glow. Paul became more alarmed because the silence was too complete. Even the jungle seemed abnormally quiet. The smell of smoke was everywhere.

"Trouble," Moonshine whispered frantically.

They continued moving along the moonlit road, keeping close to the jungle as they neared the clearing where the hospital was. Paul heard sobbing as soon as the clearing opened up before them. It sounded far away, at first, like the wailing of a small child.

He hurried onto the school grounds. The smell of smoke was stronger there, and all but one of the buildings had been bombed so that only one end of the old school building still had its walls and roof. The sobbing came from that area, and Paul and Moonshine rushed toward it. They were halfway there when the sobbing stopped. Paul cast the beam from Moonshine's torch toward the portion of the building that still stood. There was nothing to be seen but an open doorway that gaped into blackness.

"Sunday!" Paul called the boy's name several times. He listened for some response. Nothing was to be heard.

"Sunday!" he shouted again in a loud, hoarse whisper.

"Masta?" Sunday's faint voice finally came back.

Paul listened closely and stared at the building where the rustling noises were coming from.

Moonshine also heard the noises and Paul could feel him tense up at his side.

"Sunday!" Paul called out again. "It's me, Paul Jefferies."

"Masta Paul! Help!"

Paul heard movements in front of him and then he saw a figure move out of the doorway and against the side of the white building. Someone was running toward him. He turned his light on the approaching figure.

"Sunday!"

Suddenly the boy was on the ground in front of him, sobbing. Paul handed the torch to Moonshine and lifted Sunday into his arms.

"Are you hurt, Sunday?"

"Fire come and then soja come," the trembling boy cried. "I go for bush, they run to catch me."

"What about pickin'?"

"Pickin' not be dade." Sunday was sobbing loudly and pointing toward the building he had just left.

"Where are the soldiers now?"

"They go, maybe in boats. Too much trouble, masta," Sunday said.

"Where is pickin', Sunday?"

Sunday pointed again to the building where he had been hiding, and the three of them walked in that direction.

"Show me," Paul said, following the boy into the building. He heard moans from other parts of the room. He flashed the light around the room to reveal the children he had come back for. They appeared unhurt, except for their emaciated condition.

"Where is Hyacinth? Is he okay?" Paul spoke the words to no one in particular, then felt someone clutching at him in the dimness. He reached out and clapsed the young child to him.

"Hyacinth," Paul said, hugging the child and standing up with him in his arms.

"Fire no come here," Sunday said with great excitement. "Soja no boom-boom pickin'. They leave pickin'."

Left them to what? Paul wondered.

CHAPTER XVII

Bugamu, Biafra, January 13, 1970.

Paul knew that Colonel Barka and his men would return to Bugamu and he knew that the sea offered the only escape. He peered at the map on the floor of the boat in the dim light of the torch. According to the map, Calabar lay six hours or so downriver. Paul knew that Calabar was in federal hands and that there would be no help for them there, but beyond Calabar were the Cameroons and Victoria. If they could get to Victoria, he reasoned, they would be free.

Paul had come to associate the plateau with seeing Maureen again, with a feeling of hope. He often thought of the last day they had spent there together. It had been a brilliant morning, under a cloudless sky, and the air was clean and clear as he motorcycled along the serpentine road that wound up to the Hill Station Hotel. When he arrived, the desk clerk told him that Maureen was in the garden. He had a feeling where she might be so he followed the narrow path that meandered through the shrubbery and flowers and beyond the aviary to the edge of the cliff. From that vantage point one could look down at the city, itself built on hills, and enjoy the unobstructed view of the horizon.

She was seated on one of the large stones that had been set in a small semi-circle, forming a two-foot-high wall ringing the promontory. Four wooden pillars supported a small thatched roof, providing shade.

Maureen didn't see Paul as he approached for she was mesmerized by the view. She was wearing a light blue silk dress patterned with lighter flowers. The shirt had tiny, delicate pleats, and an occasional gust of wind caused it to billow, like a parachute, revealing her tanned, well-shaped thighs. Birds and the gentle rustling of wind in the trees lent music to the scene.

"Enjoying the view, I see," Paul said, sitting down.

"Oh, Paul!" She turned to face him. "It's lovely! There's nothing like this in the south." The color of the dress heightened the blue of her eyes.

He stretched his right leg toward the rock closest to the cliff and put his foot on the flat stone. He rested his forearm against his thigh and leaned forward to look down onto the city.

"Someday this will all be mine," he said, making a sweeping gesture toward the blue hills that ringed the edge of the plateau. He looked at her and smiled, waiting for her reaction.

Maureen laughed.

"Why do you do it?" she asked after a while.

"Do what?" he asked innocently.

"Pretend that you are a colonialist."

"Pretend?" he said with mock outrage.

"Colonialists, even neocolonialists, don't take their girls to native bars."

144

"Then you are my girl?"

She smiled again and said, "Be serious, Paul, Why do you do it?"

"Maybe," he said after a moment's reflection, "maybe this style of life suits me."

"But you're not really like that at all," she protested.

He didn't say anything but smiled and looked away from her to the glistening horizon.

"Do you know what I think?" she asked. "I think you act like a colonialist to mask the fact that you're really an idealist. Somehow you see that as weakness. You don't want people to think of you that way, so you put on airs."

"You think so?" He would not look at her, but he was intrigued by what she was saying.

"Your dreams for modernizing the country through telecommunications satellites don't fit the colonial pattern. I think you may even be a visionary. You have a dream for Africa, for linking all its countries through telecommunications, and you can't get much more idealistic than that!"

"I guess you know my secret," he said devilishly and looked back at her. Her words had given him a new insight into himself. "I'm in it for the money," he confessed.

"I doubt it. There're much more important reasons but you try to hide them, and I've told you that I think I know why."

Paul watched Maureen as she spoke. He had never felt about anyone the way he felt about her. To be near her was becoming the most important thing in the world for him. To be away from her was becoming unbearable.

"I have to go back tonight," she said, changing the subject and shifting her gaze from the panorama below to the flower garden that flourished next to the rock where she sat.

"Why so soon?" He was surprised by her sudden annoucement.

"Father has been called back to Lagos."

"Think you could ever live here on the plateau?" he asked after a while.

"How could anyone not like it?"

"I don't know. Some people might find it too colonial. You just associated where I live with my pretensions, didn't you? This place doesn't fit in with the new Africa."

"Perhaps not, but I sometimes wonder . . ."

"Wonder what?"

"I wonder if achieving the new Africa is worth all the suffering that's going on in Nigeria."

Paul didn't say anything, didn't move, didn't breathe. Maureen continued to surprise him with her actue sensitivity to the country's suffering. She was different from other expatriates because she was not indifferent.

"Couldn't you stay on a while longer?" He was almost begging. "Send your father on alone."

"I better not, Paul. Not this time." She tried to reassure him with a loving hug.

"We'll both be going south, then," he said, trying to sound cheerful. "You to Lagos, and I've got business near Port Harcourt."

Maureen became excited. "Oh, wonderful, Paul! When will you be leaving?"

"In about a month, I suspect. And I'll be staying down there for a couple of months, at least."

"Will you get to Lagos, do you think?" Her voice was filled with anticipation, and her question made Paul feel better about her leaving.

"Would you like that?" he asked shyly and hopefully.

"Yes, I would!" she said sincerely, returning his look. "Very much."

"Then I'll come," he said joyfully. "I'll try to come on a few weekends."

Paul took a deep breath and stretched. Maureen smiled as she watched him.

"You know what I would like?" Paul said, almost jubilantly.

"What would you like, Paul?"

"To meet here again someday. Right here, just as we are."

Maureen was stroking a large red carnation that reached over for her touch from the rock garden next to her.

"Let's meet here sometime when you are sick of living in Africa, and you long to get away. Paul was overwhelmed with excitement and he hoped to fill Maureen with the same enthusiasm.

"But this is Africa, Paul," she said quizically.

"No, it isn't, Maureen. Where you are going is Africa."

Maureen looked confused.

"That's what Hill Station is all about. It was built for expatriates like us who need to get out of the country but can't go home. In colonial days it took six months to go home to England. But you could come here for what was called local leave. It's just like the English country-side only more beautiful. In a month's time you'd be re-freshed and ready to return to the lowlands. It was a way of getting away, without really being away. It was a kind of dreamland: not really Africa and not really England either."

"A kind of dreamland." Maureen repeated the phrase to herself, and Paul could see that she was beginning to understand.

"Have you ever seen expatriates who have been in the country too long? They become hollow shells, old before their time. Sometimes they end up on booze and pills."

Maureen nodded. She had seen such people.

"Well, Hill Station reverses that process. If this place didn't exist, I would have ended up that way a long time ago." Paul smiled. "I've been saved, haven't I?"

Maureen answered him with another hug and a kiss. "Would you do something for me?" he asked seriously. "I'll try."

"Will you promise to come back here sometime? The war will be over soon. Maybe then you could stay longer. I'll be here."

"When the war is over," she said, still touching the petals of the flower, "I will come back. If you're here."

"We'll come back to this very spot," he said, patting the rock they were sitting on and pulling her close to him. "Is is a date?"

"It's a date," she promised.

Paul wanted to hurry back to the plateau so he concentrated on getting out of Bugamu. His finger followed the stretch of river on the map that led towards Andonni. Where the rivers crossed, just before the village, Paul made a mark with his pencil and followed the tributary down to where it met the sea. By taking the tributary they would bypass Calabar, and if they were lucky and didn't meet any federal gunboats, they could make a sea run to Victoria.

Paul wondered if the large pirogue could weather the trip. He flashed his light around the boat, over the six sleeping children and Moonshine and Sunday. He knew that the risks were high, but he also knew that escaping by sea was their only chance.

Early the next morning, Paul explained his plan to Moonshine. He paused after telling him that they would join the tributary to the sea at Andonni to ask, "Have you ever taken your boat on the ocean before, Moonshine?"

"Many times I go to Port Harcourt," Moonshine answered eagerly.

"That was the bay, Moonshine. Now we must sail on the ocean itself. I'm wondering if the waves will swamp the boat?"

"No swamp, no swamp!" Moonshine was happy to reassure Paul.

Paul shook his head, frustrated, and looked back at the map. He was certain that they would have no trouble getting to the sea. They would simply have to follow the river, go out maybe a quarter of a mile, and follow the shoreline. With the full moon, they would have the advantage of being able to travel at night. Accounting for fuel consumption, time and drift, Paul calculated that they could be at Victoria in about five days, if they left immediately. The thought of that picturesque city at the base of Mount Cameroon, in Man of War Bay, was like heaven to Paul, and as he folded the map and put it away, he swore that they would make it to "Heaven".

At dusk, when the bougainvilleas that lined the bank were losing their color, Paul made a final check of the boat to be sure that everything was ready. With the six children securely seated and the extra jerry can of fuel hidden on board, he pushed the pirogue into the river.

The unmistakable and reassuring smell of the sea comforted him as they traveled the tributary that led due south to open water. They had been en route for about two hours when Paul heard a strange noise. He cocked his head to listen harder.

"Moonshine, stop the engine!" he whispered. "Cut the engine! I hear something!" Paul turned from the bow of the boat where he was sitting and motioned frantically to the boatman.

Moonshine killed the engine. It coughed and gasped to a stop. The boat's vibrations ceased and suddenly all was still. Paul kept his head cocked. At first he heard only the sounds of the water lapping against the boat and the night noises of the jungle. Then he heard it again, a distant roar like the sound of rushing water.

"Moonshine, go for the bank," Paul commanded, indicating the heavy cover of darkness at the river's edge. "I hear soja boat!"

Moonshine grabbed the long pole that lay the length of the boat. He shoved it into the water, and the boat crawled toward the sanctuary of trees and overgrowth that hung over the edge of the bank. The noise grew louder with each passing second. As it got closer, it no longer sounded like rushing water but like the healthy drone of a big marine diesel engine.

Just as the pirogue slipped into the dense vegetation, the river bank became bathed in the bright white-yellow spotlights of the federal patrol boat that was rounding the bend ahead. It was a large boat and Paul could see that it carried at least two dozen soldiers. He knew they were Colonel Barka's men. The troops weren't wearing uniforms but were dressed in work clothes, and many were wearing hard hats. Each man carried an automatic rifle.

The federal boat passed within twenty feet of where Paul and the refugees were hiding. He could feel the vibrations of the heavy engines through the pirogue. Suddenly their hiding place was as light as day. Paul motioned for everyone to duck low in the boat, but he was certain that they would be discovered. The soldiers were shouting in their native dialect; they souded tense and mean. The waves created by the larger boat slapped against the pirogue, rocking it violently.

The spotlight was trained in their direction for an agonizingly long time when, just as suddenly, there was darkness again. Paul raised his head slowly to see the patrol boat moving quickly upriver. He sat up when the roar of the engines and the shouting became faint.

"We'll wait for a while," Paul whispered to Moonshine. "Maybe they'll come back. We must be extremely careful!"

They waited for what seemed to Paul a safe length of time. Finally, when the moon had risen so that it cast a silver shadow on the water and lit the landscape in a soft, luminous glow, Paul decided that the time was right.

Moonshine pushed the pirogue away from the bank with the pole, and they slid out from under the overgrowth, keeping close to the bank and listening hard for other boats. After a while Moonshine started the engine again and they moved quickly down the river. The moonlight gave them all courage, and as they rounded the bend ahead, the dank, hot air of the delta was lost in a cool sea breeze. Paul had never felt so refreshed. The air was sweet and cool, and he breathed deeply, effortlessly. He relaxed with the knowledge that they must be very close to the sea. They motored onward and Paul kept his ears trained for any foreign sounds.

The river widened and finally straightened. The silver track of moonbeams on the water lengthened and allowed Paul to see the river open into the sea in the distance.

When they were four hundred meters from the shore, which appeared as a black outline against the light water, the purple sky and the occasional white sand beaches, Paul crawled back to take control of the tiller. He set a course due east, for the Cameroons, keeping the shore on his left and the open sea on his right. The sea was calm and the pirogue was helped along by the gentle motion of the rolling waves.

They traveled at night. When the grey dawn broke on the horizon, they made for one of the many tributaries leading to mangrove. They hid themselves during the days under banks of mangrove at the river's edge. When the sun began to set, they followed its red track out onto the red wine-colored waters and reset their course for the east. The children slept most of the way, waking occasionally to drink water or to relieve themselves. Paul was thankful that Moonshine was an expert fisherman, and was able to keep them well supplied with fish during the long trip.

With the dawn of the fifth day, Paul knew that they could not be far from their destination. The landscape had changed markedly during the night; the black-green flat banks of mangrove had surrended to a mountainous shoreline. And when the grey dawn broke at last, on the sixth day, Paul saw it ahead — Mount Cameroon. The huge green base of the mountain was the only thing visible in the hazy morning light. Everything else was shrouded by the low cloud banks.

"Moonshine, we're in Cameroons!" Paul exclaimed, shaking the boatman awake.

"Sunday, wake up, we're in Cameroons!"

Sunday and Moonshine rubbed their eyes, sat up and stared in disbelief at the hugh mountain that rose directly out of the sea. The mountain formed a part of the majestic Man of War Bay, a natural harbour surrounded by mountains on all sides. As they moved closer to the shore, the mountain passed them slowly on their left and the bay opened before them. Then Paul saw the village. The sun had broken through the grey clouds, casting yellow-white shafts of light onto the tiny town. Ahead, the red-roofed rectangular buildings of the village rose in various angles to form a kind of pattern against the green mountains and the cerulean sea. Paul rejoiced, for he knew that they were out of it at last.

CHAPTER XVIII

Kaduna, North Central State, Nigeria,
February 25, 1970.

The Minister of Communications was ecstatic. "Good news on all fronts, Paul!" David Kpamba exclained gleefully. "Now that the war is over, and an amnesty has been declared, we can begin construction on the sixth earth station."

Paul had never seen his friend so ecstatic. He stood with his back to the minister, looking through the large windows of Kpamba's second-story office onto the bright, sunbathed streets of Kaduna.

"Procurement contracts for all six earth stations were signed a week before the deadline," Kpamba said. "By advising the government to authorize the sixth earth station procurement when we did, we saved the treasury five million dollars!"

Was it really only five weeks ago that he and the children had arrived at Man of War Bay in the Cameroons? It seemed a lot longer to Paul now; so much had happened. He still had not recovered from the awful reality.

He had thought that he was prepared for something like that, he had told himself a thousand times that he was, just as he did on the Cameroon Airways flight from Cameroons to Fernando Po. He knew Maureen was in bad shape when they loaded her on the plane; he knew that she might not make it. He remembered the initial flood of relief that hit him when the big door of the Cameroon Airways Fokker Friendship was opened to the rainwashed shiny black runway at Fernando Poo. Pools of water reflected the bright sunlight now breaking through the low clouds. The brightness made him squint and he couldn't believe his eyes when he saw Father Okeke standing at the bottom of the ladder waiting for him. The sight of his friend filled him with joy.

"You made it!" Paul shouted down to his friend.

"You too, Paul." The priest reached out for Paul's hand as he stepped off the ladder and onto the tarmac.

The men embraced one another heartily.

"Thank God you are safe, Paul."

"How are you, father?" Paul asked, immediately clasping the priest's hand. "I was worried about you."

Father Okeke held Paul's hand for long moment in a manner that is a natural sign of affection among African men. But his silence and his gesture was also a message. Paul was suddenly engulfed by an overwhelming sense of dread and finality. He knew what Father Okeke's reception signified.

"She didn't make it, did she, father?" Paul did not want to look at the priest. He focused on the forest at the edge of the runway.

"No, Paul," Father Okeke whispered. The priest's dark, expressive eyes were glowing with sadness. Yet, even without looking into those eyes, Paul could feel the serenity in the man.

Paul couldn't stop shaking his head. "Why, father? Why?"

"She wanted to help my people, Paul. Some people can't stand by and watch suffering. To them, that is worse than death. Maureen was such a person."

"But why did she try to do it all by herself?" Paul didn't try to hide his tears.

"Maybe for herself, Paul."

"And what did she accomplish, father? The cause is lost, the people are lost!"

"What did anyone accomplish? The pilots that flew the relief missions, the doctors, the other nurses, you, your friend Larry? There is no common answer. Each person who involved himself will have his or her private response"

"I've lost her, father, and I will never meet anyone like her again."

"Paul, you sound as though you were the only person who has lost because of this."

"Don't preach to me now," Paul said harshly, but was immediately sorry for his words. He looked his friend in the eye. "If it hadn't been for me, Maureen would never have gone into Biafra."

"No, Paul. She would have gone, no matter what. Some people are just like that. She just had to care. She would never have been happy doing nothing, just standing by." Paul could not deny the truth of his friend's words.

He looked back at the priest. "When did she die?"

"Yesterday."

Paul shook his head. He had spent yesterday making arrangements for the children he had taken to the Cameroons. He had been awake for the past twenty-four hours. He had wanted to rush back to Fernando Po but he had to make sure the children were provided for.

"If only I could have been here," Paul said, still shaking his head.

"There's nothing you could have done. I was with her and so was Larry."

"Larry." Paul looked hard at the priest. "What happened to him?"

"I think he's gone back to the plateau. He left this morning."

"Where have they taken her?"

"To the United States. The funeral will be there."

"When?"

"I'm not sure. Soon. They just took her away this morning."

"I'm going back then! I've got to be there. Do you know, if I can get a plane here somehow?" He wished they had waited so he could have made that last flight back with her. Now he would be chasing after her again. Somehow that always seemed to be the way for them.

"A plane will leave for Lagos in about an hour. From there you can get a flight back home."

Back home, the phrase sounded curious somehow.

"Let's make arrangements for your flight," the priest said and he led his friend toward the terminal.

"What?" Paul said absent-mindedly, turning around to face his friend.

Kpamba joined Paul at the window. "You were not listening, Paul. I was talking about contracts, money, progress! You were far away."

The minister sensed his friend's melancholy and waited for Paul to speak.

"Who are those people?" Paul asked after a while, still ignoring Kpamba's remarks and pointing down to a small group of men in flowing white robes. Their heads and faces were partially covered by white turbans, and each man was armed with a long rifle, a cross handled sword, and a dagger, which hung from a tightly fitting leather waist belt.

Tuaregs," Kpamba replied.

Paul had heard about the Tuaregs but he'd never seen them before.

"They're a nomadic people, very fierce. They guard caravans across the desert," Kpamba explained. "You will notice that everyone gives them their way."

"Always on the move?"

"Always."

"I'm beginning to feel like one of them," Paul muttered.

"In what way?"

"Oh, I've been living a normadic existence for years," Paul said wryly, still fascinated with the unfriendly looking tribesmen.

"But you've been here, Paul!" Kpamba said. He was concerned for his friend. "You can't compare yourself to them. They have no home. Your home is here."

"You're wrong, David. I had been away from my home for almost two years," Paul said sadly. "When I was there for Maureen's funeral, I felt out of it, like I didn't really belong any more. Something keeps drawing me back here. Sometimes I wonder if I'll ever fit in there again. Maybe I should go back and try it once more."

"But we need you, Paul!" Kpamba sounded a little frantic. "I almost forgot," he added, suddenly excited again. "I have something for you." He went to his elaborately carved teak desk, took an envelope from the top drawer and handed it to Paul with a broad smile.

"I am overjoyed to be able to present you with the deed to the land at Barakin Ladi that you asked me about some months ago. It's an inadequate token of our appreciation for all the work you have done for us. Do with the land what you like. You have the distinct honor of being one of the very few foreigners ever to be given land in Nigeria."

Paul was touched and grateful and momentarily speechless.

"I had forgotten completely about that, David," he finally said. "How on earth did you get it?"

Kpamba laughed with mock exhaustion and said, "It wasn't easy, my friend, especially since I had to tell the Ministry that I didn't know what you planned to do with it. But Mohamed Abda owed me a favor."

Paul pressed the envelope in his hands with the strength of his appreciation and slipped it into his small worn leather brief bag.

"Thank you, David," he said, shaking his friend's hand. "That is a beautiful piece of land. Maybe someday I'll build a house on it. A kind of personal Hill Station."

Paul glanced at his watch then and saw that he was late. "Oh, God, David, I've got to go! I have to catch a plane for the plateau."

"Before you go, Paul, there's something else I want to show you. I'll be quick about it."

He led Paul from his office, down to the walled back courtyard where a new, bronze-colored Mercedes Benz was parked, gleaming in the sunlight. The finish was already slightly dulled by a fine coat of dust that covered the car.

"How do you like it?" Kpamba asked eagerly.

"It's stunning, David!" Paul was bowled over by the extravagant car.

"It's mine, Paul," Kpamba said. "It's not just a car, you know. It has greater significance."

Paul's perplexed expression told Kpamba that he didn't entirely understand the nature of its significance.

"Don't you see, Paul? At last communications will be receiving the priority that it deserves. This is a gift from the government for my efforts with the sixth earth station. I owe much of it to you, Paul."

Paul smiled awkwardly, embarrassed by the compliment, and shook his head in denial.

"This is just the beginning, Paul. If you leave now, much of our work will have been wasted. We — you and I — have done the hard part. Now the government has confidence in us. Together we have convinced them of the necessity for communications development in the country. They have come to realize its importance. But we must follow the development through. You are part of it, Paul."

Paul understood the truth and importance of Kpamba's words. "But I can't make any decisions now, not yet," he said.

"Of course," Kpamba said, looking very serious for a moment.

"I have to go now," Paul said again. He clasped Kpamba's hand with both of his and then walked through the arched doorway that separated the courtyard from the street, now starkly brilliant in the sunlight.

"We have arrived, Paul! You and I!" Kpamba shouted after him. "And we must help this country arrive. You are part of it, Paul. You can't leave Nigeria now!"

CHAPTER XIX

Kuru, Benue — Plateau State, Nigeria,
March 13, 1970.

Paul had been back on the plateau about a fortnight when he received a note from Father Okeke informing him that the priest was temporarily situated at a church five miles away at Kuru. Father Okeke wrote that he wanted to see Paul as soon as he returned home. Paul welcomed the news that Father Okeke was to be his neighbor, at least for a short time, on the plateau.

Paul had also learned from his steward that during the few weeks he was in the States, Larry had also returned to the plateau and had tried to see Paul on several occasions. Each time Larry visited his house, he gave Paul's steward the address where he could be reached. When Paul returned, he ignored the messages and was careful to avoid going anywhere he might see Larry. He had heard rumors that Larry's experiences in the south had changed him drastically, for the worse. He apparently was no longer participating in the activities of his church. Paul had hoped that Larry would have taken the first available flight back to the States, but for some inexplicable reason, Larry had stayed on.

The jeep creaked and thumped as Paul negotiated the final switchback on the dusty white road that was taking him to the church where he would find Father Okeke. The deeply rutted road was fenced with tall cactus plants that marked off tiny plots of farmland. Finally the jeep topped the rising switchback, and the clearing at the top of the hill opened up. The wooden, white-steepled church he saw in the short distance would have seemed more natural in a New England village.

He parked across the road from the church, in front of the small white cottage that served as the priest's house. Father Okeke was standing on the steps of the tiny porch. He bounded across the yard as Paul climbed out of his jeep. They greeted each other warmly.

"Welcome to the plateau," Paul said.

"Thank you for coming, Paul," Father Okeke replied, ushering his friend into the living room of the small rectory.

Paul was curious about the invitation but didn't ask questions right away. He sat in an old, overstuffed chair near the only window which looked onto the church across the road.

"It's good to see you again, father," Paul said. "It's a charming church, and it makes me feel safe."

"It is lovely, but it is out of place here," the priest said, "like me."

Paul asked Father Okeke what he meant.

"This church was built by missionaries from Ireland, Paul, and it is fine for them, but I do not belong here. I came here at the end of the war because it offered temporary sanctuary. My 'fame', he spoke the words modestly" is such that my safety is guaranteed. The government is taxing to show the world that this amnesty

is genuine." But I do not plan to stay much longer."
Father Okeke paused. "My people are still suffering in
the East, and at the first opportunity, I must go back to
them."

Paul interrupted the priest. "Is that why you asked me
here today, to tell me that you're leaving soon?"

Father Okeke shook his head. "Larry has come to me
on two occasions, Paul. We are not of the same religion, as
you know, but because I was in the south, perhaps he feels
that I am closer to him than his own minister."

The priest stood still, facing Paul. He hesitated before
continuing, trying to decide if he should say what he
thought. "But I am afraid that there is not much I can do
for him."

Paul asked what was bothering Larry. Father Okeke was
quick to tell him. "He blames himself for Maureen's
death. His guilt is gnawing away at him. I am afraid it
could destroy him."

"Father, you don't know Larry very well," Paul said.
"He's much stronger than you seem to think."

"I used to think so, but not any longer, Paul. We have
met twice since the war ended. Both times he told me
what happened in Biafra and of his relationship with you
and with Maureen. He feels that you were right, that if he
had listened to you things would be very different today."

Paul could feel no sympathy. "Larry made his decision,
father," he said coldly. "He's going to have to live with it."

"Do not say that, Paul, you are judging him."

Paul was silent.

"You know, Paul, Maureen was very fond of him."

"I know."

"And she admired him."

"I'm not arguing that. He has some very admirable
qualities," Paul said, adding, "but he has rotten judge-
ment."

Father Okeke pretended he hadn't heard Paul's bitter words. "Perhaps, Paul, if you talked to him, you could make him realize that he is not as much to blame as he thinks."

"But he is," Paul insisted, "and I can't forgive him his selfishness."

"What do you gain by being bitter, Paul? He needs your help now. This is a critical time for him. If he does not get help now, I shall be very concerned for him. Paul, the man has so much talent, so much to give to this country. His skills are desperately needed now."

Father Okeke was visibly distressed. His voice trembled. He turned from Paul and moved quickly to the open doorway. Paul had not seen the priest so emotional before.

"How did Larry happen to go to Biafra?" Father Okeke asked after a while. He was staring out the doorway, at nothing in particular.

"He was in Jos, and wanted to start a clinic for the lepers. He was frustrated because he couldn't get anywhere with the idea. I told him that I'd see what I could do to get the government to help him, but that it would take time. He had no patience. The next thing I knew, he was in Biafra."

"If you could have helped him then, perhaps he would never have gone."

"Perhaps, but who can say? I did try to help him. I talked to my friend, the minister of communications, about him."

"That is just my point, Paul! Who can say who is to blame, or if there is any blame? Maureen saved my life. If I had never met her, I would be dead. Yet it was through me that she got into Biafra in the first place. Larry was just trying to help. That's all he ever wanted to do."

Father Okeke stepped toward Paul, gesticulating as he spoke. "Paul, I have a feeling about him. He is very vulnerable now. Do you think that Maureen would hesitate to help him if she could?"

Father Okeke still had the same effect on Paul. His words penetrated his being. Paul wanted to ignore what Father Okeke was saying, but he couldn't.

"I have a feeling about you, too, Paul."

"Me?"

"Are you happy?"

Again Paul remembered when Maureen had asked him that question. It was as though the priest could read his thoughts. "Sure. Why do you ask?" He tried to sound nonchalant.

"I feel that there is something disturbing you, Paul. Perhaps if you could reconcile with Larry, you would be more at peace with yourself." The priest's eyes mesmerized Paul. He thought of Maureen and his promise to her, something that he had perhaps tried to forget. The priest was waiting for him to reply.

"I can't promise anything, father." Paul got up from his chair.

"Try, Paul. That is all that I ask of you."

They shook hands.

"It is for you, too, Paul," Father Okeke whispered.

Paul moved past his friend toward the open door. He hesitated, looking at the priest.

"Let me walk you to your jeep, Paul." Father Okeke escorted him into the sunshine.

"You'll be going back, then, father?" Paul asked, relieved to change the subject as they walked.

"As soon as I can."

Going back to what? Paul wondered as he climbed into the jeep. He waved to Father Okeke and started over the switchback.

"*Ka yi na Allah,*" the Ibo priest blessed him in Hausa."

He never saw the priest again.

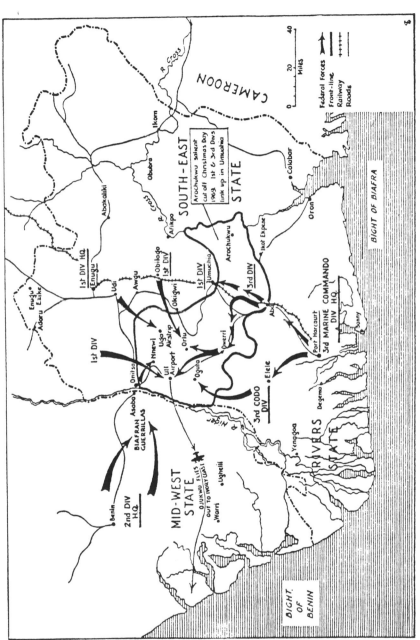

Map 12-1 • Biafra's Final Collapse, December 1969-January 1970 (from John de St. Jorre, *The Nigerian Civil War*, p. 394)

165

CHAPTER XX

Bukuru, Benue – Plateau State, April 4, 1970.

The bright sunlight flashing against the white cement sundeck next to the pool at the Hill Station Club almost blinded Paul, even with his dark glasses on. It was ten o'clock in the morning, and the part of the sky that was visible to him through the tall acacia trees was a clear blue. A cool breeze carried traces of the sweet fragrances of the hibiscus that grew in the nearby garden.

Paul was seated in his swimming trunks at a table that had no umbrella, but the breeze made him forget how hot the sun was.

The rain had finally come, and washed the skies clean of the harmattan. Paul looked over to the small pool. A six-inch-long, blue-bodied, red-headed lizard was doing push-ups on the deck. The pool water was a pale yellow that got darker as the water got deeper, so that the bottom of the pool was barely visible. Leaves, pine needles, twigs and dead bugs floated on the surface, forming little log jams of debris along the sides. The white paint on the low wall that separated the pool from the sundeck was cracked and chipping. Paul wondered what Maureen would say of the Club now: the vestiges of colonialism decaying gracefully, yet struggling to survive like some prehistoric monster that should have become extinct ages ago!

He studied his body. Five weeks of plateau sun had renewed the tan that he had lost in the south. He knew he looked good, but he would not feel good again until the thing he had to do was done.

Paul had just finished a liter of cold, strong Nigerian beer and already was feeling slightly euphoric. He had made up his mind the night before to see Larry. He didn't know what he would say to him, but he was disturbed by what Father Okeke had told him and by a gnawing feeling of guilt that he had reneged on a promise. By chance he had seen Larry walking through the marketplace in Jos the day before. He was alone and he looked terribly thin, sallow and disheveled. Larry had not seen him, but for Paul the experience had been a shock.

This day had begun strangely. Paul had retired early the night before, and it was still dark when he was a-wakened just before dawn. He had heard the cry of the muezzin calling the faithful to prayer from the neighboring compound. There had been a moment then, as he lay half asleep, listening to the call, when the feeling came upon him. It was a great awakening, as if a heavy veil had been lifted as the dawn broke. The feeling had not been altogether unpleasant, and now, as he sat under the strong sun thinking of the past few months, all that remained was a rather strange and peaceful memory, a feeling of security, a knowledge that he could accept whatever might happen with tranquility.

A young steward in a brilliant white military tunic with gold buttons approached Paul's table from the trees that hid the club buildings. He wore a large red hibiscus flower in his thick, curly black hair and carried a metal tray with one bottle of beer on it. Larry followed him down the path. The steward set the bottle of beer on the table, and Larry stood beside the table, hesitating for a moment before pulling out a chair and sitting opposite Paul.

Larry was unwashed and unshaven, and dark circles hung under his eyes. His soiled brown shirt and levis drooped on his skinny frame, and his hair was uncombed.

"I have a message for you. I tried to see you earlier but I couldn't" Larry said with no energy, shrugging his shoulders. His voice cracked and he cleared his throat. Paul was silent, but his eyes searched Larry's with a look that revealed his concern.

"It's strange," Larry continued, attempting to ignore Paul's stare. "Maureen wanted me to tell you something. She wanted me to tell you that she would meet you at Hill Station." Larry spat out the words, like someone who was carrying a heavy weight for a long time and is relieved to be rid of it at last.

The message shook Paul. He leaned back in his chair but continued to study Larry's face. Those last moments with Maureen on the plateau flashed through his mind.

"She said she had to get word to you," Larry added.

Paul looked at him in silence. There was so many questions still unanswered, and only Larry would know. After a while Larry slapped his hands on the table and stood up, sliding the chair back slowly.

"Goodbye, Paul."

The words startled Paul.

"Wait a minute, Larry, sit down, please" Paul spoke slowly, unsure of what he would say. The realization that Larry had been trying to see him for so long just to deliver Maureen's message made Paul realize that he had been unfair in his judgment of the young missionary. He had thought that Larry wanted to see him because he wanted sympathy or forgiveness.

"There's something I have to know," Paul said.

Larry slumped into his chair almost reluctantly.

"You were with her at the end?" Paul spoke hesitantly, for he knew that he would be made vulnerable by asking.

"Yes."

"Did she suffer much more?"

"She just went to sleep in the hospital at Fernando Poo," Larry answered quietly. For a moment he looked Paul in the eye.

"And she wanted me to have this message?"

"It was important to her."

Paul forced a smile at last. He asked, "You want a drink?"

"Yes, a gin and tonic." Paul was surprised at Larry's eagerness to accept the invitation to drink. Larry had always insisted on being a nondrinker.

The steward returned, took the order, bowed slightly and disappeared through the garden. Paul and Larry sat across from one another, not saying anything, for a long time.

"If only I had listened to you, Paul. If I had helped you, then Maureen would be here now!" Larry suddenly blurted out the words which Paul himself had thought so often and had planned to say. Larry's voicing them now seemed to emphasize their futility. He was a pathetic figure to Paul, as if all that he had been through in the past few months had caught up with him. He was obviously very lonely. Suddenly Paul felt only compassion for him.

"What's your plan now, Larry?"

"I don't know, Paul." Larry spoke vacantly, his eyes focused vaguely on the pool.

"Is your family still coming here?"

"I haven't been in contact with them for a while."

"Have you been working?"

"Not since I left Bugamu."

"It seems there's a lot to be done right here in Jos."

The steward set the gin and tonic on the table before Larry.

"I suppose, but somehow it's not the same. I'm afraid it will never be the same again." Larry was not a dramatic person, so the depth of despair that was revealed by his tone shocked Paul. Larry gulped a third of his drink and winced, like a man unaccustomed to liquor.

"I think you've got to try to forget about Bugamu and concentrate on the future, Larry."

"I can't forget."

"Stop it, Larry! You did an awful lot for the Ibos."

"That's not it! You know that's not it, Paul. It's Maureen."

"You're no more to blame than I am," he said after a while. His words surprised even himself.

"Don't try to humor me, Paul."

"You know, Larry, your problem is that you're so goddamned egocentric. I'm not humoring you. It's the truth."

"What do you mean?"

"Did Maureen ever tell you about our relationship prior to her going to Bugamu?"

"No. She mentioned once that she had known you before."

"Well, there was more to it than that. If it hadn't been for me, she would never have gone down there in the first place."

"I don't get it."

"She never told you that we were almost engaged, about three months before she went to Bugamu?"

"No," Larry said with genuine surprise. His eyes brightened momentarily with their old intensity.

"I walked out on her." Paul found it easy to say the words then.

"You what?"

"I walked out on her, just left."

"Why?"

"Foolishness, pride, I don't know, something very stupid." Paul shook his head and smiled ironically.

"But that doesn't make sense! It doesn't track with you coming back for her."

"Yes, it does. I originally went to Biafra for business reasons. When I arrived, things were already finished between Maureen and me. Eventually somehow we were lucky enough to get back together."

"But you did so much for the Ibos."

"I simply got involved with the program, just like everyone — you, Maureen, the people at the plantation, the pilots flying the relief missions, Father Okeke. I didn't want to leave. It was kind of an adventure."

"What are you trying to say, Paul?"

"I've said it. If I hadn't walked out on Maureen, she wouldn't have been so influenced by Father Okeke and gone into Biafra. Larry, all of us are responsible — you, me, Father Okeke, even Maureen herself."

Larry probed Paul's face, wanting desperately to believe what he heard but not yet convinced of its truth.

"What about your plan for the clinic, Larry?"

"What clinic?" Larry had genuinely forgotten his dream.

"The clinic for the leper children in Jos! I was driving through Jos the other day. They're still there. In fact, there seems to be more of them now."

Larry shook his head sadly.

"That was a pipe dream," he said quietly. "I realize that now."

"Larry, you remember that time when you came to me and asked for help in getting the land at Barakin Ladi?"

Larry nodded his head without enthusiasm.

"Do you remember the idea you had for the clinic, hoping eventually for a hospital with modern equipment?" Larry was staring vacantly at the table but Paul knew that he was listening keenly. "I've begun to realize something, Larry. You and I may belong in this country, at least for a few more years. Maybe we don't fit quite right at home."

"I don't understand."

"Well, I don't see you in some fancy practice in the States. I don't see you getting along with the AMA!"

"Perhaps not," Larry said with a grim smile. "And what about you?"

"I went back for a while, but something brought me back here."

"What?"

"Let's just say I had been happy here."

Larry nodded his understanding.

Paul opened his small leather brief bag that he had put to the side of the table. He took out a legal-size white envelope and put it on the table in front of Larry.

"What's that?"

"Let's just say it's dash," Paul said with a sly smile.

Larry touched the envelope.

"Open it," Paul commanded.

Larry opened the envelope slowly. He studied the legal document before asking, "What is it?"

"It's the deed to the land at Barakin Ladi. It's yours! Now you don't have any excuse for not beginning that clinic. I'm getting awfully tired of seeing those leper children begging on the streets of Jos. Hide them from me, will you?"

Larry looked at Paul again for a long moment, then looked away at the tapered tops of the evergreen trees that swayed gently in the breeze, against the clear blue morning sky. Tears were streaming down his cheeks. He put his head down on his arm and soon his shoulders were heaving with his sobs.

There was nothing that Paul could think of to say. He sat still for a while, feeling very awkward, surprised and shocked and saddened at Larry's despondency. He put his hand over Larry's hand and squeezed it, and they stayed like that for a long time.

GLOSSARY

Aba m bu: Ibo expression meaning "my name is."

Abinci: Hausa word for "food."

Aliekam Salaam: Response to greeting "salaam aliekam" widely used in Isamic countries and means "and peace to you."

Bakimbo: River tribe expression for white person.

Baturi: Hausa word for European.

Biafra: The Republic of Biafra was formerly the Eastern Region of Nigeria. The Republic was proclaimed on May 30, 1967 by General Odumegwu Ojukwu who was governor of the Eastern Region prior to the secession. By this act, the Republic of Biafra seceded from the Nigerian Federation. The Federal Nigerian Government considered this a rebellion. Federal Nigerian troops were sent immediately to attack Biafra.

Birom: A minority tribe in Nigeria.

Cameroon: The Republic of Cameroon or Cameroun is a country in West Africa bordering on the Northeast Gulf of Guinea. It was formerly a trust territory of France, and it shares a contiguous eastern border with Nigeria.

Caritas: Caritas Intenationales, the Catholic Relief Organization.

"Chop": British colonial slang expression for dinner.

Consul: An official appointed by a government to reside in a foreign country. The individual represents the commercial interests of citizens of the guest country.

Dai kyau: Hause expression for "very good."

"Dash": A pidgin English term for "tip and/or bribe."

Emir: An Islamic chief or prince, one who deserves great respect.

Expatriate: One who lives in a foreign country. The term is sometimes used to describe a person who has renounced his or her native country.

Fernando Po or Fernando Poo: An island off the west coast of Equatorial Guinea in the Bight of Benin area. During the Nigerian Civil War and after Nigerian federal forces captured Port Harcourt, the island was utilized as a staging area for airlifts of food and supplies into Biafra, and for medical evacuation flights out of Biafra.

Field grade officer: A commissioned officer in the army, air force or marine corps of a particular country with a rank of colonel, lieutenant colonel, or major.

Fulani: A nomadic people living in the northern part of Nigeria, and other West African countries bordering that part of the country. They are known for their physical beauty, their devotion to Islam, and their skill as herdsmen.

Gina bu aka gi: Ibo expression for "what is your name?"

Harmattan: A dust laden wind in West Africa during certain seasons of the year.

Hausa: A member of an African tribe or ethnic group who lives in northern parts of Nigeria, and other areas of West Africa which border the Northern section of Nigeria.

Ibadan: A major city in the Western State of Nigeria.

Ibo: A member of an African tribe or ethnic group living in the area near the lower Niger River. Prior to the Nigerian Civil War, it was called the Eastern Region of Nigeria and Ibos also live in parts of West Cameroon.

Ibo language: A Kwu language used as a language of trade and education in a large area of southeastern Nigeria.

ICRC: International committee of the Red Cross, comprised of Swiss citizens who have the responsibility to maintain the terms of the Geneva Convention. The organization is bound to be a neutral party in the event of war.

Independence: On October 1, 1960, Nigeria won its independence from its colonial power, Great Britain.

INTELSAT. The 108 country International Satellite Organization which provides worldwide telecommunications: i.e., telephone, data processing, and television broadcasting. (Membership number as of November 1983.)

Isak Dinesen: Pen name of author, Baroness Karen Blixen, 1885–1962. The quote at the beginning of the book is from her copyrighted work entitled Out of Africa published by Random House, Inc.

Islam: The religious faith of Muslims which considers Allah as the sole deity and Muhammad as his prophet.

Jihad: A holy war waged against those who do not believe in Islam.

Juju: A fetish, charm or amulet of West African people which is attributed with magical powers.

Kaduna: The capitol city of what was the Northern Region of Nigeria before the civil war.

Kai: Hausa expression for "how," often used as an exclamatory word. The term is sometimes followed by the "huba" for emphasis.

Ka yi na Allah: Hausa expression for "you did God's work."

Kwashiorkor: Name of a disease which literally means "red body." It is caused by severe malnutrition in infants and children who have a diet high in carbohydrate and low in protein.

Lagos: The former capitol city and port of Nigeria, on an offshore island in the Bight of Benin and on the opposite mainland.

Minister: A high officer of state entrusted with the management of governmental activities.

Mt. Cameroon: The highest mountain in West Africa with an elevation of 13 350 feet.

Meuzzin: A Muslim crier who calls out the hours of daily prayer.

Mun gode da Alla: Hausa expression for "we are thankful to Allah" in response to greetings.

Na Gode: Hausa expression for "thank your."

Nigeria: A country in West Africa bordering on the Gulf of Guinea. It was formerly a British colony and protectorate. It is the most populaced country in Africa.

Pan Africanism: A movement for greater cooperation among African nations in cultural traditions, economics, defense, and ultimately to develop a "United States of Africa."

"Pickin": A Pidgin English term for "infant" or "child."

Pidgin English: A simplified form of English used for communication among people with different languages.

Port Harcourt: A city and major port of what was the eastern part of Nigeria prior to the secession of Biafra. Subsequently, it became Biafra's major link with the outside world for food and supplies. It was taken by Federal Nigerian Forces in May of 1968.

Rebels: Reference to those pledging their allegiance to Biafra during the Nigerian Civil War.

Sabon gari: Hausa expression for "new town." Usually referred to Ibo settlements in the formerly northern region of Nigeria.

Sannu: Hausa expression for "greetings."

Sannu da aiki: Hausa expression for "how is your work?", literally, "greetings in connection with your work."

Standard earth stations: A telecommunications satellite ground receiving and transmitting facility which consists of a large dish-shaped antenna that links the INTELSAT system.

Telecommunications: Transmission between or among points specified by the user of information without change in form or content by means of electromagnetic transmission.

Telecommunications networks: Facilities such as wires, microwave towers, satellites and earth stations over which telecommunications transmissions flow.

The Nigerian Civil War: May 30, 1967 – January 13, 1970. It followed the secession from Nigeria of Biafra, formerly the Eastern Region of Nigeria, on May 30, 1967.

The Seven Sisters: The seven major worldwide oil companies.

To ranki titi: A Hausa idiomatic expression which is a response of great respect, usually used as an answer to the greeting of an emir. It is usually accompanied by a shaking of the raised fist toward the person addressed and a bowing of the head. The equivalent translation is "very good, your excellency."

Trypanosomiasis: Infection with or disease commonly called "sleeping sickness."

Tuareg: A member of the nomadic people of the central and western Sahara from Timbuktu to Nigeria. They have preserved their Homitic speech but have accepted the Islamic religion.

USAID: The United States Agency for International Development: the foreign aid arm of the Department of State.

U.S. Policy re Nigerian Civil War: The United States took a neutral position during the Nigerian Civil War, considering the war an internal Nigerian dispute.

Uthman Dan Fodio: An Islamic scholar who during the early part of the nineteenth century reluctantly became leader of a Jihad. He conquered much of what would eventually become Northern Nigeria. By his doing so, Islam became the predominant religion of that part of the country.

Yoruba: A member of an ethnic group primarily in what was the Western Region of Nigeria.

Made in the USA
Lexington, KY
22 September 2012